W9-CST-948

20 EVENTS

Inventions

THAT CHANGED MODERN LIFE

LOIS MARKHAM

RSVP

RAINTREE
STECK-VAUGHN
PUBLISHERS
The Steck-Vaughn Company

Austin, Texas

© **Copyright 1994, Steck-Vaughn Company**

All rights reserved. No part of this book may be reproduced or utilized in any form or by any means, electronic or mechanical, including photocopying, recording, or by any information storage and retrieval system, without permission in writing from the publisher. Inquiries should be addressed to: Steck-Vaughn Company, P.O. Box 26015, Austin, TX 78755

Consultant: Gary Gerstle, Department of History, The Catholic University of America

Developed for Steck-Vaughn Company by Visual Education Corporation, Princeton, New Jersey

Project Director: Jewel Moulthrop
Assistant Editor: Emilie McCardell
Researcher: Carol Ciaston
Photo Research: Photosearch, Inc.
Production Supervisor: Maryellen Filipek
Proofreading Management: Amy Davis
Word Processing: Cynthia C. Feldner
Interior Design: Lee Grabarczyk
Cover Design: Maxson Crandall
Page Layout: Maxson Crandall, Lisa R. Evans

Raintree Steck-Vaughn Publishers staff

Editor: Shirley Shalit
Project Manager: Joyce Spicer

Library of Congress Cataloging-in-Publication Data

Markham, Lois.
  Inventions that changed modern life / Lois Markham.
    p.   cm. — (20 Events)
  Includes bibliographical references and index.
  Summary: Describes twenty inventions that changed modern life, including the steam engine, photography, and television.
  ISBN 0-8114-4930-0
  1. Inventions—History—Juvenile literature. [1. Inventions—History.] I. Title.   II. Title: Inventions that changed modern life.   III. Series.
T18.M37 1994   93–17022
609—dc20   CIP
                                                          AC

Printed and bound in the United States

  2 3 4 5 6 7 8 9 0   VH   99 98 97 96 95 94

Cover: American physicist Robert Goddard (inset) launched his first liquid-fuel rocket on March 16, 1926. By doing so, he changed rocketry forever and began the expansion of the human range beyond the atmosphere.

Credits and Acknowledgments

Cover photos: NASA (background), UPI/Bettmann (inset)
Illustrations: American Composition and Graphics
Maps: Parrot Graphics

4: Library of Congress (top), Hulton/Bettmann (bottom); **5:** Paul Shambroom/Photo Researchers, Inc.; **6:** Private Collection; **7:** Ductillite is a registered trademark of Wheeling-Pittsburgh Steel Corporation. All rights reserved for Wheeling-Pittsburgh Steel (left), Will McIntyre/Photo Researchers, Inc. (right); **8:** *The Eli Whitney Gun Factory* by William Giles Munson. Yale University Art Gallery, Mabel Brady Garvan Collection; **9:** Bob Daemmrich/Stock Boston (top), Dawson Jones/Stock Boston (bottom); **10:** Library of Congress; **11:** Library of Congress (left), Japan Railways Group, Inc. (right); **12:** The Bettmann Archive (top), Gernsheim Collection, Harry Ransom Humanities Research Center, The University of Texas at Austin (bottom); **13:** Bill Horsman/Stock Boston; **14:** International Harvester; **15:** Library of Congress (top), Stacy Pick/Stock Boston (bottom); **16:** The Smithsonian Institution (left), The Bettmann Archive (right); **17:** Donald Dietz/Stock Boston; **18:** The Bettmann Archive; **19:** Courtesy Hagley Museum and Library (top), Guy Gillette/Photo Researchers, Inc. (bottom); **20:** Arthur Gerlach for *Fortune* magazine, 1936; **21:** Frank Siteman/Stock Boston; **22:** Library of Congress (top), Courtesy AT&T Archives (bottom); **23:** Spencer Grant/Photo Researchers, Inc.; **24:** Moss Photo (left), U.S. Department of the Interior, National Park Service. Edison National Historic Site (right); **25:** Susan McCartney/Photo Researchers, Inc.; **26:** The Bettmann Archive (left), Courtesy of Ruth Kravette (right); **27:** Frank Siteman/Stock Boston (left), Vanessa Vick/Photo Researchers, Inc. (right); **28:** The Smithsonian Institution; **29:** Bill Bachman/Photo Researchers, Inc.; **30:** The Bettmann Archive; **31:** Tim Holt/Photo Researchers, Inc.; **32:** From the Collections of Henry Ford Museum and Greenfield Village; **33:** Dennis Budd Grey/Stock Boston; **34:** UPI/Bettmann (left), Courtesy Arianespace (right); **35:** NASA; **36:** The Bettmann Archive (left), The Bettmann Archive (right); **37:** Bob Daemmrich/Stock Boston; **38:** University of Chicago Library (left), *The Birth of the Atomic Age* by Gary Sheehan/Chicago Historical Society (right); **39:** UPI/Bettmann; **40:** Courtesy Hagley Museum and Library; **41:** Stacy Pick/Stock Boston (top), David Parker/Photo Researchers, Inc. (bottom); **42:** Charles Gupton/Stock Boston (top), The Bettmann Archive (bottom); **43:** Will and Deni McIntyre/Photo Researchers, Inc.

10676

Contents

NORTHMOUNT SCHOOL LIBRARY

Steam Engine 4

Food Canning 6

Interchangeable Parts 8

Locomotive 10

Photography 12

Combine Harvester 14

Sewing Machine 16

Refrigeration 18

Plastics 20

Telephone 22

Electric Light 24

Automobile 26

Radio 28

Airplane 30

Assembly Line 32

Rocket 34

Television 36

Nuclear Fission 38

Computer 40

Laser 42

Glossary 44

Suggested Readings 46

Index 47

Steam Engine

A new source of energy began the Industrial Revolution.

While repairing a Newcomen engine, James Watt saw ways to improve it. By adding a separate condenser, Watt eliminated the need to reheat the steam cylinder.

Natural Power

For centuries, the only power available to human beings was provided by nature. The energy needed to get work done came from wind (windmills), flowing water (water mills), or muscles—either human or animal. But these energy sources had drawbacks. Wind was unpredictable. Flowing water was found only in certain places. And muscles get tired and need to rest.

As early as the first century A.D., a Greek scientist named Hero had made use of another source of energy—steam. In Hero's *aeolipile,* water boiling in a suspended sphere pushed steam into two tubes. As a result, the sphere revolved in a manner very much like a modern lawn sprinkler. It was the first steam engine. However, Hero developed no practical uses for his scientific novelty.

Steam to the Rescue

Much later—in 18th-century England—Thomas Newcomen, an ironmonger, produced the first practical steam engine. Newcomen had built it to solve a problem that tin miners were experiencing: the deeper they mined, the more the mine shafts filled with water. Newcomen's machine could pump the water out of the mine shafts. He offered tin miners his machine in 1712, but they were not interested. It would cost too much to buy and transport the coal needed to run the engine.

Undaunted, Newcomen took his steam-driven pumping engine to the coal miners, who had the same need as the tin miners—as well as an unlimited supply of the fuel needed to run the engine. The coal industry became the first to use the steam engine on a large scale.

Newcomen's engine produced a steady pumping action that helped remove water from mines.

Watt Builds a Better Steam Engine Newcomen's steam engine worked, but it was far from efficient. It consumed vast amounts of coal and was very slow. Still, it was all that was available for more than 50 years. Then in 1764, Scottish engineer James Watt was given a Newcomen steam engine to repair. Examining the engine, Watt began to understand what made it inefficient. In Newcomen's engine, a cylinder fitted with a piston was filled with steam and then injected with cold water to make the steam condense. This created a vacuum that pulled down the attached arm of a pump. The cylinder then had to be reheated to steam temperature for the cycle to start all over again. Watt saw that much time and energy could be saved by condensing the steam in a closed vessel separate from the cylinder. Thus, the cylinder would always remain hot and would not have to be reheated. Improving the efficiency of the steam engine increased its usefulness, even when fuel was expensive.

Watt built his first improved steam engine in 1768 and patented it in 1769. But it wasn't until 1775 that Watt's steam engine was produced for sale. Over the years, Watt continued to make many improvements in the design of the steam engine. Perhaps the most significant was changing the back-and-forth motion of a piston in a cylinder to a rotary motion that could move wheels. This innovation dramatically increased the number of uses for the steam engine. The steam engine was quickly adapted for use in a steam carriage for roads. It was built in 1769 by Nicholas Joseph Cugnot, a Frenchman. In England, Richard Trevithick built the first steam locomotive in 1803.

In compressors and pumps, which need abundant supplies of steam to operate, steam engines are still being used.

It's a Revolution!

More than any other single invention, James Watt's improvements in the steam engine brought about the Industrial Revolution. This term refers to the dramatic change from an agricultural economy to a manufacturing economy that began in England in the late 18th century, reached the United States in the mid-19th century, and is still spreading throughout the world.

Perhaps the most significant effect of the steam engine was that it replaced waterpower in factories. This meant that factories no longer had to be built next to rivers. Thus, factories sprang up everywhere, creating employment for more people. As more people moved to be near the factories, villages became towns, and towns became cities. In fact, the entire landscape of several countries changed completely. In addition, a higher rate of employment increased the general level of income. More money meant that more people could feed and house themselves better. This, in turn, meant that more people—especially infants—lived longer, and the population increased.

The steam engine enabled manufacturers to produce many types of goods more quickly and cheaply. Transportation became more efficient as inventors found ways to use the steam engine to run ships and locomotives. Even when inventors harnessed the power of electricity, it didn't replace steam, which was still needed to generate large amounts of electricity.

The Disadvantages The Industrial Revolution was a mixed blessing, however. The cities that sprang up around factories were often overcrowded and polluted. More children survived infancy, but they were put to work at an early age in factories that were unhealthy and unsafe. People's capacity to earn money was limited by frequent economic depressions that threw them out of work. Still, there was no stopping the revolution. And the very evils that it produced gave rise to reformers determined to make the world a better place for those who toiled in it.

Food Canning

A contest resulted in a new method for the preservation of food for future use.

The Challenge

Food spoils for two reasons. First, the chemicals that help fruits and other foods to ripen continue working after the food is ripe. Eventually these chemicals cause the food to go bad. Second, microorganisms—molds, yeasts, and bacteria—in the air attack food and cause it to spoil.

For thousands of years, people preserved many foods by drying, pickling, salting, and smoking. However, these methods produced a monotonous and often inadequate diet for sailors, soldiers in the field, and others who did not have access to fresh food.

In the 1790s, the French general Napoleon Bonaparte faced the problem of finding a dependable source of food for his army as it conquered Europe. Napoleon offered a prize of 12,000 francs to anyone who could develop a method for preserving meat and vegetables for a period of several months.

Pasteur proved conclusively that bacteria, not air, were responsible for food spoilage. His method of sterilization—called pasteurization—destroys the bacteria, but not the flavor.

The Challenge Met

Scientists had been at work on the problem for many years. In 1740, British naturalist John Turberville Needham tried heating mutton broth in a jar to preserve it. A few days later, when he observed microorganisms in the broth, Needham concluded, wrongly, that the bacteria would simply appear on their own.

Italian biologist Lazzaro Spallanzani questioned Needham's methods. In 1768, he repeated Needham's experiment, boiling the food longer than Needham had. He found that no new organisms appeared. His conclusion was that bacteria in food could be killed if the food was heated long enough and at a high enough temperature. This work laid the scientific groundwork for someone to take up Napoleon's challenge. That man was Nicolas Appert.

The Winner Appert, a Parisian candy maker, began experimenting with food preservation in 1795. By sealing food in wide-mouthed glass bottles and heating the bottles in boiling water, Appert discovered that he could preserve a variety of foods, including meat, vegetables, fruits, milk, and eggs. By 1796, Appert had closed his candy shop and left Paris. His goal was to improve his methods

and win the 12,000 francs. In 1804, he opened a bottling factory in Massy. Several years later, Appert loaded 18 different bottled foods onto a ship called the *Stationnaire*. When the bottles were opened five months later, the food was unspoiled. Appert won the prize!

Following Appert In 1810, Appert published a book about his methods. Within a year, British engineer Bryan Donkin read the book and offered Appert a thousand pounds for detailed instructions in his method. Donkin then improved the process by raising the temperature during boiling. Donkin and his business partners made another improvement. They put the food in tin-plated cans, which were more durable than Appert's glass jars. The firm of Donkin and Hall soon became the suppliers of tinned foods for the British navy.

The Benefits of the Tin Can

By the early 1820s, tin cans of preserved food were readily available in England, where the name of the container was shortened to *tin*. The new method also spread quickly to America, where the container was called the *can*. Whatever they called it, people agreed on the benefits of canning:

- People could transport food over long distances.
- A greater variety of foods was available during nongrowing seasons.
- Canning assured a reliable food supply when there were shortages of fresh fruits and vegetables.

One unexpected benefit was that some women now had to spend less time in the kitchen preparing food.

Going Further Although canned foods were widely available by 1860, the process was still not completely understood. Many people thought that the most important part of canning was the removal of air from the container rather than the heating of the food. French scientist Louis Pasteur proved conclusively that the opposite is true. Pasteur heated food to a high temperature and then left it in an open jar shaped like a swan's neck—curving down and then up.

With this jar, air could reach the food, but dust and other impurities were trapped in the curve of the jar's neck. When the food did not spoil, it was clear that it was the bacteria, not the air, that caused food to spoil.

Pasteur also applied Appert's methods to the preservation of liquids. He found that bringing wine to a high temperature destroyed its good taste. At a lower temperature, however, the organisms were killed but the flavor remained. This process of heating liquids to delay spoilage is known as *pasteurization* in the French scientist's honor. It is used for a wide variety of foods, including milk.

Canned foods—fruits, vegetables, meats, and other foods—still occupy supermarket and home shelves.

This 1940s advertisement urged people to buy canned foods because cans preserved the freshness and flavor of foods, and they were easily disposable.

Interchangeable Parts

An American manufacturing system used unskilled labor to assemble uniform, machine-made parts.

At his factory in Connecticut, Whitney used his "uniformity system," in which power-driven tools produced identical parts, to manufacture 10,000 muskets for the U.S. government.

Making Guns by Hand

Today people value—and pay more for—items made by hand. Whether modern craftspeople blow glass, hand-tool leather, or knit one-of-a-kind sweaters, they are admired for their skill. Their products are valued because good handmade articles are rare.

But there was a time, less than two hundred years ago, when everything was made by hand. There were few factories and no assembly lines or machines for mass-producing everyday items from pots and pans to work boots. Highly skilled craftspeople worked many hours to produce one-of-a-kind products. No two items were ever exactly identical.

Two hundred years ago, for example, each part of a gun was made by hand, and then all the parts were assembled by hand. Therefore, if one part broke, it could not be replaced by the same part from another gun. In the heat of battle, this was a serious disadvantage.

In the late 18th century, soon after the American War of Independence, bad feelings between the new nation and France threatened to erupt into war. The United States needed a large supply of guns—and fast. But who would make them?

The American System

Whitney's Idea The man who got the contract to produce 10,000 muskets for the U.S. government in 1798 was the American inventor Eli Whitney. Whitney was well known for inventing a device that completely changed the cotton industry in the South. He had been visiting in Georgia when he learned that the production of cotton was limited by the difficulty of separating the cotton fibers from the seeds. He set to work and quickly devised a cotton gin that could do this. However, although Whitney patented his invention in 1793, others used his design without paying the royalties due him. Whitney received little financial reward for his efforts.

When war with France threatened, Whitney sought the contract to produce the 10,000 muskets. To get the job done quickly, his idea was to use precision machinery which could more accurately do the work previously done by craftsmen.

Besides speeding up the production of guns, Whitney's new system also produced guns with uniform, interchangeable parts. The parts could be assembled by unskilled workers, each of whom was trained to do one small part of the job.

A famous story is told about Whitney. To demonstrate the merits of his new manufacturing process, he dumped the parts from several disassembled guns in front of a government official. Randomly choosing one

8

People have always been willing to pay more for certain handcrafted items, such as musical instruments. This craftsman is making dulcimers.

of each part, he quickly assembled the pieces into a finished product.

Guns and Everything Else The war with France never materialized. But Whitney's system of using precision machinery to create products with interchangeable parts soon became standard practice. It was used in the production of office and agricultural machinery, sewing machines, and firearms. In 1851, at London's Great Exhibition, European engineers wandering through the exhibits were astounded by the precision and efficiency of the goods produced in America. Soon they were calling the new system of standardized parts production and assembly "the American system of manufacture."

When the Civil War broke out in 1861 and large numbers of firearms had to be produced quickly, America's manufacturing industries changed over to mass production using Whitney's methods.

America's Industrial Revolution

It soon became apparent that large factories using unskilled labor were cheaper to run than small workshops that employed skilled craftspeople. Furthermore, because machine-made parts were produced faster than hand-made parts, Whitney's system increased the output of goods. The new system was changing the United States from an agricultural economy into a manufacturing economy. It was America's Industrial Revolution.

A New Labor Force There were many who were unhappy with the new American system of manufacturing. Artisans and skilled workers lost work because their skills were no longer in demand. Eventually their craft unions—early labor unions for particular trades—broke up. The new work force of largely unskilled laborers had trouble organizing unions because they did not have a common skill to bind them together.

At first America's unskilled factory workers were generally exploited by factory owners and industrialists. Eventually, they began to organize to fight for their rights. By doing so, they created a strong American labor movement.

Although mass production eliminated some jobs, it created many others. The need for unskilled labor was greater than ever before. And in the last decades of the 19th century, immigrants looking for work came to the United States in greater numbers than ever before to fill that need.

Many everyday items, such as compressors for air conditioners, are assembled more cheaply and efficiently using interchangeable parts.

Locomotive

The "iron horse" spurred economic growth and changed the way people and products moved from place to place.

By Land or by Sea

Movies about the past might lead you to believe that traveling on horseback or by stagecoach was a dashing, romantic way to get about. But in reality, travel by horse was strenuous, dirty, and often dangerous. Dirt roads were littered with tree stumps, deeply rutted from the constant use, and muddy after rains. "Corduroy" roads, which consisted of logs laid sidewise, hurt horses' legs and bounced wagons to pieces. And travelers were easy prey for robbers.

Travel by water was another option. Travel by canalboat or steamboat was more pleasant than horseback or stagecoach. But water travel was slow, and waterways didn't go everywhere. Until the early 19th century, horses and boats were the only ways to move people and products from one place to another. As the world became more industrialized, a strong need for fast, inexpensive transportation developed.

A Series of Improvements

Steam Power Railroads first appeared in England in 1597 when horse-drawn carts, traveling on wooden rails, carried coal from nearby mines to the Trent River. More than a century later, the invention of the steam engine presented a new possibility for moving goods by rail. However, the first steam engines didn't generate enough power to move large vehicles.

In 1798, English engineer Richard Trevithick built a powerful, high-pressure steam engine. Nearly six years later, he put that engine in the first locomotive to run on iron rails. The engine pulled five loaded coaches a distance of nine and a half miles at a speed of nearly five miles per hour. However, that speed was still slower than a horse's.

The Rocket Another Englishman, George Stephenson, took up where Trevithick left off. By 1825, Stephenson had increased the speed of the locomotive by adding tubes that recycled the steam. His first locomotive pulled 38 cars at a speed of 12 to 16 miles per hour.

However, England was still not convinced that the locomotive was the wave of the future. A contest was proposed to test the practicality of various steam locomotives. In 1829, George Stephenson's son Robert handily won the contest with the *Rocket,* a locomotive that achieved a speed of 26 miles per hour. At last, overland transportation faster than a galloping horse was a reality!

Railroads Take Off The locomotive, nicknamed the "iron horse,"

By using tubes to recycle the steam, Stephenson increased the capability of the earlier locomotive.

became an immediate success. In Great Britain, the Liverpool and Manchester Railway opened in 1830. And the first underground railway was built in London in 1863.

In the United States, the South Carolina Canal and Rail Road Company began operating the country's first regularly scheduled steam locomotive, the *Best Friend of Charleston,* on Christmas Day in 1830. It ran between Charleston and Hamburg, South Carolina. By 1850, there were 9,000 miles of rails in the United States. And by 1880, there were 93,000 miles of track. By the late 1800s, railroads stretched across the entire country. The first transcontinental railroad was completed in 1869 when the Union Pacific and the Central Pacific met at Promontory Point in Utah and officials drove a golden spike into the last tie with a silver sledgehammer.

Japan's railroad system is the busiest in the world. The *Shinkansen,* or bullet train, carries thousands of passengers daily, at speeds of over 100 mph. France's *TGV* broke the speed record with a run of 320 mph in 1990.

Changing America

Railroads created an economic revolution. Agricultural products and manufactured goods could be carried faster and more cheaply by rail than by land or by water. As goods became available to more people, the demand for everything—from fresh fruit to firearms—increased. The result was a rapidly expanded economy. Nowhere was this more obvious than in the United States.

Adapting for America Although the locomotive had been created in England, American engineers soon began adapting it for use in the United States. They developed bigger and more powerful engines that could pull more cars. They added headlights for safer night runs, cabs for drivers to sit in, and cowcatchers to remove obstacles from the tracks. George Westinghouse developed the air brake, a safety feature that made it possible to stop the locomotive and the cars behind it simultaneously.

Railroads Change America The railroads opened up the Great Plains and the Rocky Mountain plateau to

settlers, who could not have survived in these places without supplies delivered by rail. However, what was good for the settlers was disastrous for Native Americans. The onslaught of settlers drove the Plains Indians from their homelands farther west into the territory of other Native Americans. Railroads also hired hunters to kill buffalo to clear the way for the railroad, and for their hides. Huge herds of buffalo that the Plains Indians depended on were destroyed. In 1865, an estimated 12 to 15 million buffalo roamed the plains. By 1883, they were virtually gone.

Big Business Railroad companies were America's first large corporations. Railroad executives were management pioneers, developing methods for operating large companies. By 1906, two-thirds of U.S. rail miles were under the control of seven large groups. But if business owners found strength in size, so did railroad workers, who staged the first nationwide labor protests in 1877. It was the first hint of the growing power that organized labor would wield in the next century.

First class train travel was comfortable, safe, and luxurious. One could leave Washington in the morning, dine in Philadelphia in the afternoon, and arrive in New York in time for supper.

11

Photography

New techniques for the old camera produced permanent images of reality.

In a Dark Room

For thousands of years, the only way to create a picture of reality was through painting or drawing. But the accuracy of such images depended entirely on the skill of the artist. Then along came the first camera. It was a room with a small hole in one wall. Through the hole, full-color images of reality passed from outdoors to the opposite wall.

As far back as the 10th century, Arab astronomers used the *camera obscura* ("dark room" in Latin) to view eclipses of the sun. Much later, the device was used by artists to achieve realistic drawings by tracing the outlines of objects seen through a camera.

Over the centuries, inventive souls improved on the camera obscura. A convex lens (one that curves out like the surface of a sphere) placed at the hole in the wall made the image larger. A mirror turned the image right side up. A diaphragm—an adjustable lens opening—sharpened the image. Eventually, the room was reduced to a box that could be carried around. However, one drawback remained. The images obtained with the camera obscura were not permanent. When the source of light disappeared, so did the images.

Add Some Chemicals

Around 1800, Thomas Wedgwood, son of the famous English porcelain maker Josiah Wedgwood, experimented with using chemicals to fix permanently on paper the images captured by a camera obscura. Although the idea was good, Wedgwood failed because the chemicals he used were not sensitive enough.

The first to succeed where Wedgwood failed was French physicist Joseph-Nicéphore Niepce. In 1826, he made a lasting image from a camera obscura using chemicals. But the method wasn't perfect: the image had to be exposed for eight hours, and the process produced only one copy of each image.

Daguerreotypes By 1837, another Frenchman, Louis Daguerre, had reduced the exposure time to less than half a minute. He then changed the

The early camera obscura was a darkened room with a small hole in one wall and the viewer inside the room. The later camera obscura was a box: the image was reflected right side up through glass onto the underside of the paper, enabling the artist to trace the image.

◄ Matthew Brady—perhaps the first photojournalist—organized a corps of photographers to visually record the Civil War. His portable "studio" contained a darkroom and photographic supplies.

design of the camera and experimented with different chemicals. Daguerre's improvements captured the attention of the world. Soon daguerreotypes, as his photographs were called, became the rage among scientists, artists, and the general public. Between 1840 and 1860, millions of daguerreotypes were made. Each one was unique. However, there was still no way to produce multiple copies of an image.

Negatives and Other Positive Developments

The next great leap came in 1839 when Englishman W. H. Fox Talbot created a transparent negative of an image. When light was passed through the negative onto a paper treated with chemicals, the result was a positive image. There was no limit to the number of positives that could be made from a photographic negative. Talbot also reduced the exposure time needed to a second.

Scottish physicist James Clerk Maxwell took the first color photograph in 1861, though it wasn't until 1935 that Kodachrome color film made color photography widely available.

For years photography was a complicated procedure that could be executed only by professionals. But in 1888, American industrialist George Eastman offered his easy-to-use Kodak camera to the public. The days of amateur photography had begun.

The World Made Small

Photographs made the world smaller by allowing people to see things that previously they could only read about or see in drawings. Portrait photography became immediately popular. Abraham Lincoln believed that he won the election of 1860 in part because of a widely circulated portrait of him by the famous photographer Matthew Brady.

Brady was one of an expanding group of documentary photographers. While Brady chronicled the American Civil War, Edward Curtis and others captured images of Native Americans in the West before their way of life was destroyed. Later Jacob Riis took photographs to document the crowded conditions in the New York City slums.

Other photographers, such as Ansel Adams and Alfred Stieglitz, were less interested in documenting reality than in investigating the artistic possibilities of photography. Their work created a brand-new field of visual art.

While documentary and art photographers explored with their cameras, the general public was having fun. By 1888, consumers could buy a Kodak camera loaded with a roll of film that would take 100 pictures. When all the film had been exposed, the user shipped the camera back to the factory. There the film was unloaded and developed, and a new roll was inserted. The camera and photographs were sent back to the customer. It was easy and relatively inexpensive. In 1900, 100,000 Americans owned Kodak cameras. By the 1940s, most Americans owned cameras. And in the 1980s, amateur American photographers shot an average of 10 billion photos per year.

Photography inspired other inventions. In 1889, the technology of still photography led to the development of motion pictures. Polaroid produced the first instant camera in 1947. And the photocopying machine, which has become a necessity in today's offices, made its appearance in 1950.

Despite television's instant communication, photographers still try for that one perfect picture "worth a thousand words."

Combine Harvester

A new machine reduced the number of laborers needed to harvest grain and enabled farmers to produce larger harvests.

Down on the Farm

No work is more essential than feeding the world's population. For thousands of years, this important work required huge investments of human and animal labor. Men, women, children, and animals worked long and tedious hours in the fields to ensure that there was enough food for the next year. In fact, producing food required the labor of much of the world's population. In 1790, for example, about 95 percent of the population of the new United States was involved in agriculture. The average small farmer in the United States produced enough food to feed his family.

By the beginning of the 19th century, farm production had increased considerably. This was due in part to better plowing and planting techniques. However, the gain in production seemed to exaggerate the inefficiency of the harvesting process.

Bringing in the Harvest The demand for farm labor was greatest at harvest time. Grain, like many other crops, ripens quickly and because bad weather can easily ruin a whole crop, large numbers of workers and animals were needed to bring in the harvest quickly. Looking for ways to speed up harvesting, several people had developed simple reapers—devices that could cut grain as they were pulled or pushed across a field. However, in the days of plentiful and cheap labor, such machines were not considered necessary. They offered no real advantage to farmers.

The United States Changes During the 19th century, however, changing conditions in the United States made it necessary to replace human labor with mechanical farming devices. For one thing, the Civil War and an expanding number of factory jobs took laborers away from farming. An ever-increasing urban population created a growing demand for food. In addition, the size of the average farm increased as pioneers began to settle vast new fertile areas in the Midwest. Finally, better farming technology—plowing, sowing, and hoeing devices—facilitated larger harvests. These conditions created an urgent need for mechanical farming and harvesting aids.

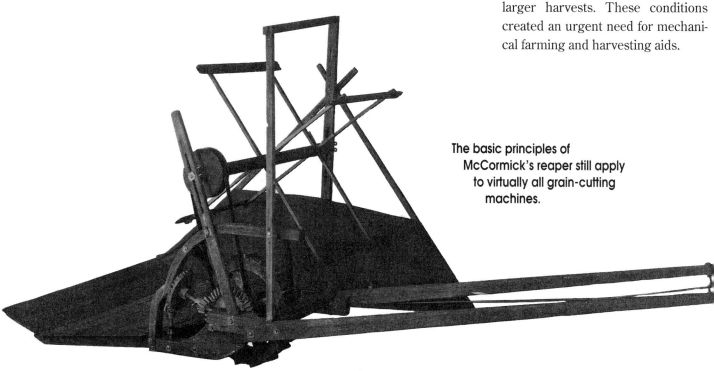

The basic principles of McCormick's reaper still apply to virtually all grain-cutting machines.

The early combine harvester was heavy and needed a team of horses to pull it across a field. Later improvements on the harvester included steam-powered and gas-powered machines.

One Machine, Two Jobs

For thousands of years, farm workers harvested grain the same way: they walked through the fields with long curved-bladed instruments, called scythes or sickles, cutting the grain as they went. Other workers followed behind bundling the sheaves of grain. Robert McCormick thought there had to be an easier way. For 15 years, he tried unsuccessfully to build a workable mechanical reaper. In 1831, his eldest son, Cyrus, then 22 years old, succeeded where his father had failed. In Cyrus McCormick's reaper, a sawlike knife dragged across a field cut the crop, which fell onto a platform on the rear of the reaper. Pulled by horses, McCormick's earliest reaper could do the work of five farm laborers. In 1851, a mechanism was invented that held the cut grain until enough had been collected to make a sheaf. In 1878, a mechanical twine knotter, which tied the sheaves, was added to the reaper. One reaping machine could then do the work of 40 people in the field.

More Work to Be Done Even with the mechanical reaper, there was still much work to be done by hand. The grain had to be cut from the stalk and then separated from the husk. Separating the wheat from the husk was accomplished by a beating motion called threshing. The next step in the mechanization of the farm was a machine to do the threshing. Simple threshing machines had also been around for centuries, but as with reaping machines, an abundant labor supply made them unnecessary. In the 1830s, Scotsman Andrew Meikle developed a successful threshing machine. It was practically ignored in Great Britain because threshing by hand gave winter employment to workers who would otherwise have to rely on charity. It was much more popular in the United States.

Combine and Conquer If a mechanical reaper and a mechanical thresher were desirable, imagine what a boon it would be to combine the two into one machine. In 1835, A. Y. Moore attempted just such a combination—but with little success. Then in 1910, the Canadian firm of Massey-Harris produced a horse-drawn combine harvester that resembled the modern machine. A few years later, steam-powered and gas-powered machines became available.

Less Work, More Food

The combine harvester greatly reduced the amount of labor needed to harvest crops. As a result, many farm workers left rural areas in the 1920s and moved to cities to find work in manufacturing.

Farms, meanwhile, were yielding bigger and bigger harvests. Soon the United States was not only feeding its growing population, it was also exporting grain to other nations. As a result, farming became big business, especially in the American Midwest. Small farms found it increasingly difficult to compete with their giant neighbors.

With agriculture fully mechanized, scientists have turned their attention to developing hardy disease-resistant crops. This has been especially important to developing nations that are still barely able to produce enough food to feed their ever-increasing populations.

Combines revolutionized farming—from the small family farm to the gigantic agricultural corporations.

Sewing Machine

A new mechanical device radically reduced sewing time.

Howe's machine sewed a double-threaded lock stitch with a needle having an eye at the point—features found in many machines today.

First, the Needle

Sewing began in prehistoric times with the invention of the needle—a pointed tool with a hole called an eye on one end. Scientists have found large numbers of eye needles made of mammoth tusks, reindeer bone, and walrus tusks in caves where people lived 40,000 years ago.

As significant as the eye needle was, sewing tasks remained time-consuming and tedious for thousands of years. Less than 200 years ago, it took 14 hours to sew a shirt by hand. In the home, women and girls spent much of their time sewing clothing for the family. Outside the home, men, women, and children labored long hours for low wages in crowded, unsafe factories called sweatshops. In the United States, many of these workers were immigrants who could not find work elsewhere.

In the 19th century, an expanding world population created a growing demand for clothing. In addition, both France and the United States had large numbers of soldiers to outfit with uniforms and footwear. The time was ripe for an invention that would speed up the process of sewing.

Many Inventors Try

In 1825, a French tailor named Barthélemy Thimonnier invented a machine that sewed a chain stitch. Each stitch passed through a loop in the previous stitch, thus making stitches that were easy to pull out.

For a time, workers in Thimonnier's factory in Paris operated 80 of his machines making uniforms for the French Army. However, angry tailors, fearful that the new machines would put them out of work, twice wrecked the factory.

A New Place for the Eye At about the same time that Thimonnier invented his chain-stitch sewing machine in France, a New Yorker named

The manual for Singer's early machine suggests that the machine was so easy to use that, with Mother's careful supervision, even a child could learn.

Walter Hunt built a machine with several features of the modern sewing machine. For example, the needle had an eye near the point, and the machine sewed a lock stitch. That is, a thread in the needle formed a loop and a second thread was pulled through the loop by a shuttle. The lock stitch will not unravel as easily as Thimonnier's chain stitch. Despite the improvements he made, Hunt never applied for a patent.

Howe's Race Credit for the first successful sewing machine goes to Elias Howe of Massachusetts. Unaware of Hunt's work, Howe invented a machine that sewed a double-threaded lock stitch with a needle having an eye near the point. To demonstrate the speed of his machine, Howe set up a race between his machine and five experienced seamstresses sewing by hand. His machine easily beat them.

Howe received a patent for his machine in 1846. However, it had one serious drawback. The cloth to be sewn was held on pins extending from a metal strip that moved with each stitch. When one length of seam had been sewed, another section had to be attached to the pins.

The Singer Sewing Machine In 1851, Isaac M. Singer took out a patent on a machine that eliminated the flaw in Howe's machine. Singer was a mechanic who held patents on several other inventions. Asked to repair a sewing machine, he studied it carefully and within a few days had improved on the original design. Singer's machine was operated by a treadle, or foot lever, which made it easier to use. The needle moved up and down in a straight line, and the cloth lay on a plate that moved forward after each stitch.

At about the same time, Allen Benjamin Wilson was also making improvements on the sewing machine. Eventually Howe, Singer, and Wilson joined all of their patents and worked together until the patents ran out in 1877.

More for Less

In the late 1860s and early 1870s, designers of women's clothing responded to the new invention by making fashions more elaborate and detailed. Even with a sewing machine, the new fashions required much labor. So for a while, the sewing machine failed to save homemakers any time at all. However, styles eventually became simpler and the sewing machine truly became a labor-saving device.

Sewing machines revolutionized the garment industry. Mass production made clothing, shoes, and leather goods more affordable. A shirt that once took 14 hours to produce could now be made in an hour. Naturally it cost less and was available to more people.

In addition to making major improvements in the machine, Isaac Singer changed the way some products were sold in the United States. Singer hired 3,000 traveling salesmen to sell his sewing machines door to door. Some of his salesmen even carried the news of his machines to distant countries, including Russia. He also allowed customers to pay for his machine in installments, an incentive that was—and still is—hard for buyers to resist.

Although some machines are run by computers, many clothing factories still have sewing machines operated by people.

Refigeration

Mechanical means of cooling made it more convenient to preserve fresh food.

Ice was sold by weight and deliveries were made frequently, especially during the summer months.

The Iceman

A hundred years ago, if you walked down a residential street on a warm summer day, you would probably see several houses with a sign in a window reading ICE in large letters. Eventually, a horse-drawn truck would pull up to one of these houses. A man would jump down and with large tongs lift a huge block of ice from the truck and take it to the back door. Once in the kitchen, he would put the ice in an insulated icebox. The home icebox, where perishable food could be kept from spoiling for a short time, had some disadvantages. The ice had to be replaced frequently and was messy when it melted. But it was a definite improvement over the communal icehouse—an underground pit or cellar where huge blocks of ice cut from ponds in winter were insulated with a covering of straw or sawdust.

Keeping food cold is one method of preserving it so that it doesn't spoil or cause illness in those who eat it. So it's not surprising that inventors were eager to find a way of refrigerating food—a method that would eliminate the mess and inconvenience of natural ice.

Looking for a Cool Gas

In 1755, Scottish chemist William Cullen made ice by mechanical means. Using a powerful vacuum pump, he brought about the rapid evaporation of water. The heat needed for the evaporation was absorbed from the water, lowering its temperature and making it freeze. However, this proved to be an inefficient method.

In the 1830s, several inventors accomplished mechanical cooling using liquefied gas. Scientific investigations had shown that if a liquefied gas was allowed to evaporate, it would lower its own temperature and also the temperature of anything around it. Repeatedly condensing a gas (making it liquid) and allowing it to evaporate (become a gas again) would remove heat from a refrigera-

tor and let it escape into the surrounding air.

Ether, Ammonia, and Freon In 1834, American inventor Jacob Perkins, working in England, patented the use of the gas ether for this process. According to one story, when Perkins' assistants first succeeded in making ice by this method, they wrapped a small amount in a blanket and carried it across London by cab to Perkins' home to show him. Perkins was by that time advanced in years, and he never developed his invention into a marketable product.

Credit for the first marketable refrigerator goes to James Harrison, a Scot who had emigrated to Australia. Harrison was a printer and is said to have noticed the cooling properties of ether while washing type with it.

18

This early advertisement emphasizes the health benefits of refrigeration.

The type became very cold when the ether evaporated. Harrison built an ether refrigerator, which was displayed at the International Exhibition of 1862 in London. Harrison was aware of the potential profits that could be made by transporting Australia's abundance of food to Great Britain, where it was sorely needed. In 1873, he attempted to ship meat to England but failed.

In 1870, German physicist Karl von Linde used the same technique but substituted ammonia for ether. Linde also marketed his refrigerators, but because ammonia is poisonous, they weren't considered safe enough for home use and were used only for industrial purposes, such as meat packing and ice making.

In 1930, American chemist Thomas Midgley developed a non-flammable, nonpoisonous coolant called Freon, which made it possible to put a safe refrigerator into homes.

Refrigeration Spreads

Even before home refrigerators, industrial refrigeration was changing the way America ate. Used in railroad cars and ships to transport food long distances, refrigeration made fresh fruits and vegetables available year-round in cold climates. Refrigeration also meant that foods could be stored for longer periods.

By the 1930s, refrigerators were a standard feature in the kitchens of most homes. Gone were the mess and unreliability of the old icebox. The new refrigerator greatly increased the variety of foods and beverages available to most families.

Further Developments Keeping foods cool was only the beginning of the refrigeration revolution. Early in the 20th century, American Willis Carrier applied the process to keeping people cool. The result was air-conditioning, which today can be found in office buildings, factories, cars, and any other places that heat makes uncomfortable.

In the 1920s, Clarence Birdseye took the refrigeration of food one step further. He used the available technology to develop a method of quick-freezing food for preservation. With Birdseye's method, some foods could be kept for even longer periods. Birdseye's work was the beginning of today's giant frozen-food industry.

The Future of Freon Thomas Midgley's 1930 discovery, Freon, is still used in refrigeration today. However, its future is in doubt. Freon is one of a group of compounds called chlorofluorocarbons. For years, scientists believed that these compounds did not react with other elements. However, it is now known that they do undergo reactions in the upper atmosphere. Thus they are contributing to the breakdown of the ozone layer, the atmospheric layer that protects the earth from harmful ultraviolet rays of the sun. Researchers are now looking for alternatives to Freon. So far, nothing has been found to replace it.

The refrigerator and freezer sections in modern supermarkets offer a wide variety of foods to consumers.

Plastics

**Through advances
in chemistry,
a new family of
materials was created.**

The Billiard Ball Challenge

Imagine a computer carved out of stone, a steel bicycle helmet, a glass toothbrush! Imagine a world without plastic.

Until the middle of the 19th century, every manufactured item was made from natural materials—wood, stone, metals, ivory, ceramics, glass, or natural fibers.

Some of these materials were abundant and readily available. For example, sand—the main component of glass—can be found almost everywhere.

Other natural materials, such as metals, were scarce, difficult to get, and expensive. Even back in the mid-1800s, before the world cared about endangered species, the ivory used to make piano keys and billiard balls was hard to come by and very costly. That is why Phelan and Collender, a New York City company that produced billiard balls, offered a prize of $10,000 to anyone who could develop a substitute for ivory.

The Birth of Plastics

In the 1830s, scientists had begun experimenting with carbon compounds, which are large molecules containing the element carbon. One such experiment yielded a substance called pyroxylin, a combination of cellulose and nitric acid, which was useful in the newly developing science of photography. Pyroxylin was one ingredient of a syrupy liquid called collodion, which contained the light-sensitive chemicals needed in photography.

John Wesley Hyatt, an American printer and inventor, responding to the billiard ball challenge, began

**While looking for a better
billiard ball, scientists created a
whole new family of materials.**

experimenting with pyroxylin and camphor, another carbon compound. By combining these substances under heat and pressure, Hyatt produced celluloid, the first plastic, which he patented in 1869.

Celluloid was first used to make billiard balls, of course, and dental plates (the holders for false teeth). But before long, Hyatt was busy marketing his new discovery for the manufacture of combs, piano keys, shirt collars, and knife handles. Later refinements in celluloid made it suitable for camera and motion picture film.

Versatile Bakelite Forty years passed before another plastic was invented. But they were busy years, especially for the Belgian-American scientist Leo Baekeland. Arriving in the United States in 1889, Baekeland soon made his fortune by inventing the photographic paper Velox, which he sold to George Eastman, the inventor of the Kodak camera.

With the proceeds from the sale, Baekeland built a laboratory on his estate in Yonkers, New York. There he began experimenting with phenol and formaldehyde. One result looked like a promising substitute for shellac. And it was while pursuing this idea in June of 1907 that Baekeland invented the second plastic, which he promptly named Bakelite.

Bakelite was both stronger and cheaper to make than celluloid, and it could be formed into more shapes. Perhaps its greatest advantage was that it did not conduct electricity or heat. Therefore, it was soon being used as an insulator in radio cabinets, door handles, pot handles, and camera cases.

A Plastics Explosion In the mid-1930s, a number of new plastics were developed. Wallace Hume Carothers invented nylon, the first plastic that could be made into fibers. The first nylon stockings were produced in a laboratory in 1937 and appeared in department stores three years later. Approximately 64 million pairs were sold in the first year.

Other plastics developed in the 1930s include polyvinyl chloride (used in tablecloths, shower curtains, floor covering, and phonograph records), polystyrene (used in hair curlers and radio and TV cabinets), polyethylene (used for toys, raincoats, and telephone cable coverings), and acrylics (used for TV screens and safety goggles).

By using plastics and recycling them, we help conserve natural resources and protect the environment.

Plastic Everywhere

Can you look around you today without seeing plastic? The 20th century has become the age of plastics. Following the surge of new plastics in the 1930s, the shortage of metals during World War II made plastics extremely popular.

Today chemists can adapt plastics to fill a wide variety of needs. Plastics can be strong and hard or lightweight and soft. They can be colorful or clear, flexible or firm. In all, about 60 plastics have been developed. They are found everywhere—in clothing, toothbrushes, packaging, toys, and automobile parts.

By replacing natural materials, plastics help conserve resources such as wood, stone, and metal. Recycling plastics can help conserve the petroleum and coal resources used to make them. Using plastic parts in cars can even help conserve fuel, because lowering the weight of a car reduces the amount of fuel needed to run it.

COMMON PLASTIC MATERIALS

Name	Uses
Acrylics	Windows, automobile rear lights, textiles
Cellulose Propionate	Telephone housings, pens, typewriter keys
Epoxies	Flooring, electrical hardware
Phenol Formaldehyde	Electrical parts, pot handles
Polyphenylene Oxide	Machine parts
Polysulphone	Battery cases, smoke alarms, shower heads

This is just a partial listing of plastic materials and their uses. Look around you for more ways in which plastics are used.

Telephone

As human voices traveled over wires, instant person-to-person communication became a reality.

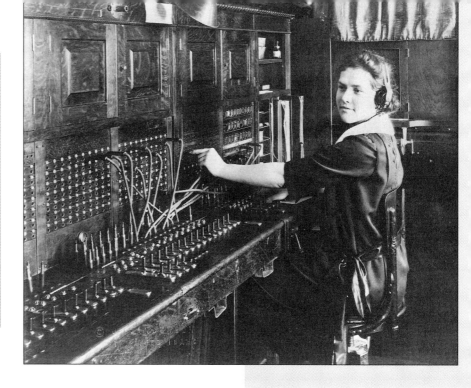

Telephone services provided job opportunities for women—and economic independence.

Drums to Dots and Dashes

The human urge to communicate has been overcoming time and space for centuries. Drumbeats and smoke signals, carrier pigeons and semaphore flags have been used to send and receive messages.

As methods of communication became more sophisticated, postal services were about the best way of delivering messages. That is, until 1844. In that year, Samuel F. B. Morse successfully demonstrated the telegraph. Using electrical signals over wires, Morse sent his now famous message—"What hath God wrought!"—from Washington, D.C., to Baltimore, Maryland, a distance of 40 miles. Within the next 12 years, Morse and his telegraph had become famous throughout North America and Europe. Telegraphs were first used to report the positions of ships and trains, and later to send private messages to and from telegraph offices. Messages were sent in *Morse code,* a system that used dots and dashes to represent the letters of the alphabet. By 1854, telegraph wires spanned the United States.

Singing Wires The next step was sending human voices over wires. In 1860, German physicist Philip Reis made an early experiment in this area when he built a device that could send musical notes a short distance over wires. A year later, he sang songs that were received—although imperfectly—100 meters (about 110 yards) away.

In 1892, Bell generated much excitement by making the first long-distance call from New York to Chicago.

So the Deaf Might Hear

The man who first sent human speech over wires was actually looking for a way to help deaf people. His name was Alexander Graham Bell. Bell's father was a teacher of the deaf, and when the family emigrated from Scotland to Canada in 1870, Bell joined his father's profession. Before long, Bell had moved to Boston to teach and do research.

Interested in developing an efficient hearing aid, Bell explored every possible connection between electricity and acoustics, the science of sound. While working on a device to send several different messages simultaneously over the same telegraph wire, Bell discovered that different tones varied the strength of an electric current in a wire. As he put it, "If I could make a current of electricity vary in intensity precisely as the air varies in density during the production of sound, I should be able to transmit speech telegraphically."

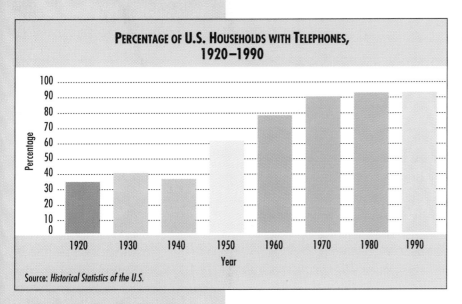

PERCENTAGE OF U.S. HOUSEHOLDS WITH TELEPHONES, 1920–1990

Source: *Historical Statistics of the U.S.*

Modern phone systems are completely electronic—connections are made automatically.

The telephone was an instant hit. Its popularity continues to grow as new phone products, such as mobile phones, are introduced.

Bell built a microphone with a membrane that would vary an electric current and a receiver that would reassemble the variations into recognizable speech.

On March 10, 1876, Bell and his assistant, Thomas A. Watson, were setting up equipment when Bell spilled acid on his trousers. He called out, "Mr. Watson, come here—I want you." Watson, on another floor, came running. He had heard the words over the primitive telephone. Bell's call for help was the first telephonic message.

Ironically, another American inventor, Elisha Gray, applied for a telephone patent just two hours after Bell did. However, the U.S. Supreme Court eventually awarded the patent to Bell.

Bell's telephone was far from perfect, and another famous inventor, Thomas Edison, improved on it. In 1877, Edison developed a carbon button for the microphone, which improved the transmission of sound.

The Bell System

The telephone soon became much more than a novelty. In 1878, the first manual telephone exchange, with women as switchboard operators, opened in New Haven, Connecticut. By 1885, telephone lines connected New York and Boston. In 1915, Watson and Bell placed the first long-distance call across the continent. In 1923, the first transatlantic call—from New York to Britain—was made. And four decades later, in 1962, a satellite named *Telstar* made possible transatlantic telephoning without wires.

Big Business   Telephone business became big business. Alexander Graham Bell's father-in-law, Gardiner G. Hubbard, organized the first Bell Telephone Company. Within a few decades it had merged with other telephone companies to form the American Telephone and Telegraph Company (AT&T), still a giant in the communications field.

People Will Talk   The telegraph had to be operated by a specialist who understood Morse code, but just about anyone could use a telephone. As a result, the telephone became a

fixture in many homes. In 1880, 54,000 homes in the United States had telephones; by 1890, 234,000 had phones; and by 1910, the number had risen to 7.6 million.

In addition to helping families and friends stay in closer contact, the telephone also stimulated the economy. With faster communication available, many companies expanded beyond their immediate area to do national and even international business.

The telephone—along with the typewriter—also helped make some women economically independent. By opening up new opportunities for women to work outside the home as switchboard operators, the telephone provided a way for more women to earn their own income.

And What of Bell?   Although Alexander Graham Bell became a very rich man, he continued his scientific experiments in many areas and never gave up his work on behalf of deaf people. In 1890, he founded the Alexander Graham Bell Association for the Deaf. And it was to Bell that the parents of the blind and deaf Helen Keller first took their child for help.

23

Electric Light

⊠

A series of inventions made the world a brighter place.

Using information from the findings of other scientists, Edison and his assistants succeeded.

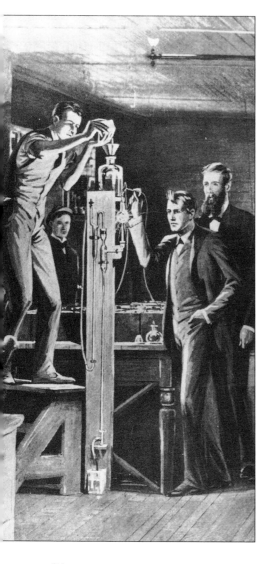

Let There Be Light

The 19th century had many ways of lighting up the indoors after nightfall: a roaring fire; the soft glow of candlelight; kerosene, oil, and—the newest technology—gas lamps. Yet even with all of these illuminating devices, it tended to be gloomy inside after dark.

However, starting around 1800, a series of discoveries about electricity caused excitement. People wondered about its potential uses—especially as a source of lighting.

First, in 1800, Italian scientist Alessandro Volta developed an electric battery capable of generating flowing electricity. Then, in 1820, Danish scientist Hans Christian Oersted made the connection between electricity and magnetism by showing that a magnetic field surrounds wire carrying an electric current. Just one year later, in England, Michael Faraday demonstrated that a magnet will produce an electric current if it is moved close to a wire. His discovery is the basis for all electric generators.

By mid-century, much had been learned about electricity, but the question remained: how to harness electricity to light up homes?

Inside the Bulb

The first electric lights were arc lights. They were developed by Sir Humphrey Davy in 1809, although they were not in general use until 1852. Arc lighting occurred as a brilliant flash of light between two carbon rods carrying an electric current. Noisy, smoky, and requiring much attention, they were mostly useful for lighthouses and streetlights.

To those working on the problem of electric lighting, incandescent light showed much more promise than arc lights. *Incandescent* (from the Latin word meaning "to shine") refers to light created by electrically heating a filament (a thin material that is capable of conducting electricity) inside a glass bulb.

The Three Challenges There were some technical roadblocks in the development of incandescent lighting. First, air inside a glass bulb causes a filament to burn up in a short time. So an improved

◀ A replica of the first incandescent light bulb can be seen in the reconstructed Menlo Park Laboratory in Dearborn, Michigan.

COMPARING LIGHT INTENSITY		
Type of bulb (100 watts)	Number of lumens	Number of candles
incandescent	1,600	127
fluorescent	7,800	620
sodium lamp (used for street lighting)	9,500	756
Source: Illuminating Engineering Society of America Handbook.		

means of removing air from the glass bulb was needed. This problem was solved in 1865 by Hermann Sprengel's vacuum pump.

The second challenge was finding the right substance for the filament. It had to be something inexpensive that could withstand high temperatures without melting. In December 1879, English chemist Joseph Swan demonstrated the first light bulb using a carbon filament in a vacuum. However, Swan did not patent his invention and did not get the bulb into production until 1881.

In the meantime, American inventor Thomas Alva Edison and the "Edison Pioneers," as he called his associates, had been working on the same problem. In October 1879, Edison produced his first successful light bulb using a scorched cotton thread as a filament. The bulb burned for 40 hours. Unlike Swan, Edison patented his light bulb immediately. Lewis H. Latimer, an African American engineering expert, was one of Edison's original team. He later wrote the first book to explain the use of the electric light.

Edison also set about solving the third challenge: developing a large-scale source of electricity. With money from wealthy investors, Edison personally supervised the construction of the first public system to generate electric power. The Pearl Street power station opened in 1882, supplying electricity for New York City's Wall Street district.

◄ A lumen is a standard unit of measurement of light intensity: a candle placed in the center of a sphere with a diameter of one foot emits 12.57 lumens of intensity.

In addition to providing light, modern lighting is used for decoration and for attracting attention. The Ginza, Tokyo's principal shopping and entertainment district, is shown here.

A Brighter World

The filament light bulb would bring electric lighting into homes, offices, and factories, and the demand for it was great even from the beginning. In 1882, Edison's Pearl Street power station supplied electricity for 2,323 lights. In 1884, it fueled 11,272 lights; by 1885, it lit 250,000.

Providing electricity was soon big business. In 1883, in order to avoid conflicts over who owned which patents, Thomas Edison teamed up with Joseph Swan to form the Edison and Swan United Electric Light Company, Limited. Eventually this partnership became the well-known General Electric Company.

Brighter, Safer, and More Fun

Electric lights changed people's lives dramatically. Better illumination inside after dark meant that people could accomplish more both in their homes and in their places of business. Outside, electric lights provided greater illumination on roads, so that people could travel more safely after dark.

Electric lights weren't just safe and convenient. They were fun, too.

Electric lights were used to decorate stores, advertise brand names, and provide a festive atmosphere for outdoor celebrations. In 1915, the San Francisco–Panama International Exposition featured spectacular displays of lights. Searchlights, colored lights, and lights imitating the aurora borealis (northern lights) introduced the wonder of electric lighting to visitors from around the world. President Woodrow Wilson opened the exposition by throwing a switch in Washington, D.C., that turned on the lights in San Francisco—more than 3,000 miles away.

Later Developments There was still plenty of room for experimentation in the brand-new field of electric lighting. Around 1910, the tungsten filament was developed. Tungsten, a very strong metal, could be operated at higher temperatures than any previous filament. In the 1930s, fluorescent lighting—cheaper and longer-lasting than incandescent lights—appeared and soon became popular in schools, offices, and factories. And in the early 1930s, neon lights gave a whole new look to city streets.

Automobile

The "horseless carriage" changed the way Americans worked and played.

Improvements made cars bigger and better, quieter and faster. This Chevrolet ad appeared in a magazine in 1957.

Chevy puts the purr in performance!

The dashing new Corvette (left) and the Bel Air Sport Cou...

On Foot or on Horseback

Imagine the streets of your community empty of cars. A century ago, if you lived in a small town, you might see a few horse-driven buggies traveling along the muddy, rutted dirt roads. Generally, however, when people wanted to get around town, they walked. For longer journeys, they traveled by train or steamship. But

Henry Ford takes a drive in his first automobile. Although based on Benz's design, the early Ford cars were much less expensive.

trains and ships ran on schedules that might not match a person's needs.

As early as 1769, inventors had been trying to develop something to replace the horse and buggy. In that year, French engineer Nicholas-Joseph Cugnot built a steam-powered, three-wheeled vehicle. It was different, but not an improvement. It was neither faster nor more convenient than a horse, since water had to be boiled to produce steam.

Then in the mid-1800s, internal-combustion engines appeared on the scene. Powered by a mixture of gas and air, they avoided the boiling-water problem of the steam engine. When German engineer Nikolaus Otto built an improved internal-combustion engine in 1876, there was finally a light, efficient, and powerful motor that could be used for personal transportation.

A Three-Wheeled Wonder

Karl Friedrich Benz, a German engineer, worked for a locksmith. But he spent his spare time designing "horseless carriages." Benz had developed his own simple internal-combustion engine. However, he soon gave it up in favor of Otto's better engine.

In 1885, Benz built the first successful gasoline-driven automobile. It was a three-wheeler that used the Otto engine and reached a speed of nine miles per hour. And it contained many features that became standard in later automobiles. It had a carburetor to vaporize the fuel, an electric ignition, and a radiator to cool the engine.

In 1890, Benz built a four-wheeled car that he displayed in the United States a few years later. This vehicle inspired the twin brothers J. Frank and Charles E. Duryea, bicycle mechanics from Massachusetts, to build the first successful American gasoline-powered automobile in 1893. In 1895, the Duryeas won the first automobile race in the United States. A year later, they sold the first car in America.

Cars for the Masses

Although the first horseless carriage was built in Europe, the United States pioneered the mass production of cars. The nation was a vast landmass with many isolated communities that were eager for easier access to the nearby towns and cities. In addition, people in the United States had higher average incomes than Europeans. Ultimately, however, it was the inspiration of one man that made cars available to the masses of Americans.

The Ford Phenomenon Henry Ford built his first car in 1893, basing his design on Karl Benz's original model. However, while Benz and other European carmakers continued to build expensive models that only the rich could afford, Ford turned his attention to making inexpensive and reliable cars that would appeal to the average American.

In 1908, he introduced the Model T, a simple, no-frills car that Americans

The popularity of the automobile eventually created traffic jams that have become a part of life in and around big cities.

affectionately nicknamed the Tin Lizzie. The first Model T sold for under a thousand dollars. But that price didn't satisfy Ford. He continued to experiment with cost-cutting ideas. In 1913, he installed a moving assembly line in his factory, cutting the production time from 12 hours per car to 1.5 hours.

The moving assembly line enabled Ford to manufacture more and more cars every year. Increased production and sales resulted in lower car prices. In 1924, Ford sold 2 million cars at the all-time low price of $290. Henry Ford also raised his workers' wages and, in the process, placed car purchases within the reach of millions. In 1914, for example, he began paying assembly-line workers $5 a day—almost double the average wage in American manufacturing. More than anyone else, Henry Ford made Americans mobile.

The Car Culture Ford may have put a car in every garage, but other car companies kept Americans coming back for newer models. In 1927, General Motors introduced the yearly model change, an idea that has come to be known as planned obsolescence—deliberately making things that will go out of style so that people will buy newer models.

The automobile changed the face of America. Existing roads and highways were paved and improved, and new highways were built. Cars also changed the way Americans lived,

As concern for natural resources grows, scientists are developing alternative fuels. This bus uses methanol, a compound used in automobile antifreeze.

worked, and played. Since people could now live farther away from their jobs, suburbs sprang up around the cities. The architecture of the homes changed as the garage became a desirable feature. Car owners, no longer dependent on train routes and schedules, could travel to more remote spots for vacations and recreation.

America's increasing reliance on automobiles also stimulated the steel industry, which supplied the metal used for car parts, and the petroleum industry, which manufactured the gasoline for car engines.

What's Good for America? As cars became bigger, faster, and more essential to the American way of life, their disadvantages were revealed. Polluted air, clogged highways, and oil shortages eventually led to smaller, more economical cars. But some environmentalists see the need for even more radical change. In recent years, there have been pleas for Americans to reduce their dependence on cars and rely more on mass transportation.

Radio

Sounds traveling over the airwaves brought about a new entertainment industry.

Over the Air

Imagine the world before radio or television. What did people do for information and entertainment? In the early years of the 20th century, if you wanted information and news, you read. For entertainment, you could also read, or you could attend social gatherings, lectures, vaudeville shows, plays, and concerts. However, an invention was coming that would change that dramatically.

In 1888, German physicist Heinrich Hertz discovered the existence of radio waves, which could relay signals without wires. Eight years later, 20-year-old Italian student Guglielmo Marconi was investigating the practicality of using radio waves to communicate over long distances. Marconi discovered that reception of a radio signal was better if vertical wires were attached to the transmitter and the receiver. Thus, in 1895, he invented the antenna. By 1897, Marconi had sent radio signals to ships 18 miles at sea.

In 1897, Marconi (*standing*) transmitted signals to a tugboat 18 miles away. Within a few years, Marconi's "wireless" equipment was in use on many ships.

From Signals to Voices

Marconi's moment of triumph came on December 12, 1901, when he sat at a receiver in Newfoundland, on the coast of Canada, and picked up radio signals sent from the coast of England. Transatlantic communication—without the use of wires—was a reality. The age of radio had begun. Still, messages were sent in coded form, not by voice.

However, on Christmas Eve, 1906, another breakthrough occurred. Canadian Reginald Fessenden, transmitting from Brant Rock, Massachusetts, broadcast the first program of music and human speech over radio waves. The cost was high and the quality was low, and not much attention was paid to the event.

The problem with early radio was that signals were weak and hard to hear. In 1907, Lee De Forest produced a device that could amplify the sounds coming over radio waves. He didn't publish his research until 1913. In 1916, De Forest broadcast the first radio newscast when he announced the results of the presidential election.

Land and Sea, War and Peace

Ships were first to take advantage of the new technology and installed the wireless devices so that they could communicate with one another at sea. When the ocean liner *Titanic* hit an iceberg and sank on April 15, 1912, the ship nearest to it was unaware of the tragedy because the radio operator was off duty. As a result, ships soon employed round-the-clock radio shifts.

World War I put great emphasis on developing the military potential of radio, although messages were still sent in code. After the war, commercial radio developed rapidly. The first scheduled broadcasting stations—one in Pittsburgh and another in Detroit—were on the air in 1920. During the decade, the number of stations increased dramatically. The airwaves became so crowded, in fact, that the signals of smaller stations were overwhelmed by the signals from larger ones.

Eventually, the owners of radio stations joined together to form networks of allied stations. NBC was formed in 1926, CBS in 1927, and MBS (Mutual Broadcasting System) in 1934. Looking for ways to increase profits, radio stations began to carry on-air advertising. Nationwide networks with their access to a vast number of consumers were a brand-new means for advertisers to bombard the public with their messages. At first, there was resistance among listeners. To some, advertising represented an invasion of privacy. But the networks found a way around this. They had their entertainers—singing groups, bands, and comedians—take the names of sponsors. For example, a national chain of supermarkets was represented by the A&P Gypsies.

Radio Mania Radio became a major source of family entertainment. Listeners could remain in the comfort of their own homes and enjoy comedy, drama, thrills, and chills. In 1922, 60,000 Americans owned radios; in 1930, almost 14 million did.

During the day, homemakers tuned into serial dramas called "soap operas" because they were generally sponsored by soap manufacturers. In the late afternoon, children home from school listened to adventure shows written specifically for them— "The Green Hornet," "Superman," "The Lone Ranger," and others. In the evening the whole family gathered around the radio set to listen to comedians George Burns and Gracie Allen trade quips or to thrill to "Buck Rogers in the 25th Century." The situation comedy "Amos 'n' Andy" was so popular that when it was on many movie theaters stopped their films and turned on radios so audiences could listen to the show.

News shows were also popular, and when World War II broke out in Europe in 1939, radio brought the war into American living rooms with Edward R. Murrow's riveting broadcasts from war-torn London.

Going On By the 1950s, television had begun to replace radio as a major source of information, news, and entertainment. However, new developments ensured that radio would remain a popular source of music. In 1948, the transistor allowed for the production of miniature portable radios. And in the 1960s, stereophonic broadcasts—making radio music almost as good as live performances—made radio even more appealing.

Early radios were large, cumbersome, and full of tubes and wires. The newest ones don't even need batteries. The radio shown here is powered by the sun.

GROWTH OF RADIO OWNERSHIP AND STATIONS, 1930–1990		
Year	Number of U.S. Households with Radios	Number of Radio Stations
1930	13,750,000	618
1940	28,500,000	847
1950	40,700,000	2,144
1960	50,193,000	3,483
1970	62,000,000	4,228
1980	78,600,000	7,871
1990	92,800,000	9,244

Source: *Statistical Abstracts.*

Despite the arrival of television, the popularity of radios and the growth of radio stations continues to the present.

Airplane

⊗⊗⊗

Humans flew, and the
world became a
smaller place.

NEW YORK TO PARIS SINCE 1927			
Model	Flight Time (hours)	Aircraft Capacity	Year Service Began
Ryan NYP *Spirit of St. Louis*	33	1	1927
Lockheed L-1649	12	75	1957
Boeing B-707	7	163	1958
Boeing B-747	7	345	1970
British Aerospace/ French *Concorde*	3½	100	1977

In 1927, Charles Lindbergh flew from New York to Paris in just over 33 hours. Advances in airplane technology made the trip shorter and more comfortable.

On the Wings of Birds

Fascination with flight goes far back in human history. Artist and scientist Leonardo da Vinci (1452–1519) drew designs for a flying machine based on his study of birds. However, those adventurers who attempted to fly in ornithopters—machines that imitated the flapping wings of birds—failed, often with loss of life or limb.

The first real breakthrough in human flight came when British inventor George Cayley figured out that flight in a heavier-than-air machine was possible. In 1804, he built the first model glider based on the aerodynamic principles he had formulated.

An early attempt at powered flight took place in 1890 when French inventor Clément Ader built a steam-powered airplane that flew for 165 feet. Unfortunately, Ader could not control the plane.

Between 1891 and 1896, German engineer Otto Lilienthal built and flew the first full-scale glider. Lilienthal was killed in a glider crash in 1896, but his designs greatly influenced two American brothers, who were soon to be airborne.

Human beings have always been fascinated by flight. This drawing of a flying machine was made by Leonardo da Vinci about five hundred years ago. He based his designs for this and other flying machines on his studies of birds.

The Wrights' Experiment

Wilbur and Orville Wright, owners of a profitable bicycle shop in Ohio, had followed with interest the glider experiments of Otto Lilienthal. After the German aviator died, the Wrights devoted more and more of their time to studying the problems and possibilities of human flight.

Serious by nature, the Wrights approached the problem in a systematic way. They studied the flight of birds, noticing that buzzards twisted their wingtips to keep their balance, and guessed that aircraft could be stabilized in the same way.

They also studied the work of others who had thought about the problem of flight, and they experimented with kites and gliders. When their experiments revealed that much of the information they had been working with was wrong, they built a wind tunnel to conduct their own research on aerodynamics.

By 1902, the Wrights had built and piloted a glider that they could easily control. The next step was to add power to the glider. The Wrights thought that a gasoline engine would be the best, but they could not find one that suited their needs. So they designed and built a four-cylinder, 12-horsepower gasoline engine. They also designed and made a propeller.

Today's supersonic transport (SST), traveling faster than the speed of sound, makes the trip from New York to Paris in less than four hours.

Airborne! Late in 1903, Orville and Wilbur Wright were ready to try out their aircraft, which they had named *Flyer.* From Dayton, Ohio, they transported their plane to Kill Devil Hill near Kitty Hawk, North Carolina. On December 17, Orville took off from the top of a dune and flew for 12 seconds. They flew three more flights that day, with Wilbur and Orville taking turns as pilot. The best flight of the day lasted 59 seconds and went about 825 feet. By the end of the day, the Wright brothers had become the first humans in history to make sustained, controlled flights in a heavier-than-air machine. A measure of their achievement was that *Flyer* did not just sail down a hill. The ground where it landed was as high as the ground from which it took off!

Improvement and Growth

For the next five years, the Wrights continued to experiment and improve on their invention. Because they held no patents or contracts to produce airplanes for money, they didn't make any public flights until 1908. But during this period, they were increasing the flight time—the time the plane could remain in the air. When they did go public in 1908, the plane, *Flyer III,* carried a passenger for the first time. *Flyer III* could stay aloft for about two hours and 20 minutes.

Moving Along Airplanes and flight developed rapidly. By 1914, planes could reach speeds of 126 miles per hour. During World War I, airplanes were important weapons of war—useful for gathering information about enemy activities even if they were incapable of sustained battle. It wasn't until World War II that airplanes truly changed warfare.

Between the two wars, in 1927, American flyer Charles Lindbergh thrilled the world when he made the first solo flight across the Atlantic Ocean—from New York to Paris—in the *Spirit of St. Louis.*

In 1933, the Boeing 247 became the first modern airliner, carrying ten passengers and two crew members. It was quickly followed by larger and faster planes.

By the 1950s, large commercial jets were replacing propeller planes. These planes carried twice as many passengers and flew twice as fast as propeller planes. Another significant milestone occurred in 1947, when American test pilot Charles Yeager broke the sound barrier by flying faster than the speed of sound. By 1970, a supersonic transport, the *Concorde,* was regularly traveling faster than the speed of sound as it carried passengers between America and Europe.

NORTHMOUNT SCHOOL LIBRARY

Assembly Line

A new manufacturing technique speeded up production time and lowered costs.

Made by Hand

The word *manufacturing* comes from two Latin roots that mean literally "to make by hand." And for thousands of years, craftspeople did make everything—from toys to drinking mugs—by hand. It was a time-consuming and expensive process, and only the wealthy could afford to own anything beyond the bare necessities.

Then in 1798, American inventor Eli Whitney used precision machinery to make interchangeable parts for muskets. The parts were assembled by specialized, though unskilled, workers. The result was faster production and less expensive products. The process was soon adapted to the manufacturing of a wide variety of products.

A century later, when the first automobiles were made, they were produced one at a time. Only the rich could afford them. However, in 1904, Ransom E. Olds decided to use interchangeable parts in his one-cylinder Oldsmobile. By doing so, he produced five thousand cars in a year. But even with interchangeable parts, automobiles were still expensive to produce—until Henry Ford got into the auto business.

The Line that Changed Manufacturing

Henry Ford was a dreamer, but a hard-working one. Raised on a farm in Michigan, he had no liking for the drudgery of farm work. He did, however, enjoy tinkering with things. In 1893, at the age of 30, Henry Ford built his first automobile. And he started his own company six years later. His dream was to build a reliable car that the ordinary person could afford to own.

Ford took the first step toward realizing his dream when he introduced the Model T Ford motorcar in 1908. To keep down the cost, the car's design was simple, and it was available only in black. The Model T sold for about $950—much less than other cars of the time. But that was still a large sum of money for most people.

A Car a Minute Ford didn't give up his quest for a cheaper car. By 1913, with the Model T still selling strongly, he installed a moving assembly line in the Ford factory at Highland Park, Michigan. The automobiles moved along on a conveyor belt one-fifth of a mile long. At each step of the manufacturing process, a worker, with the necessary parts and tools, performed a single part of the car's assembly before the car moved along to the next work station.

Conveyor belts were not a new idea. In the 19th century, they had been introduced for transporting goods in ports. The first large one was installed in Liverpool, England, in 1868, to move grain. Chicago meat packers introduced them in their plants to speed the process of "disassembling" slaughtered cows and pigs. However, Henry Ford was the

At the end of the assembly line at Highland Park, Model T bodies slid down a chute and were carefully placed onto the chassis—the frame, wheels, and machinery.

first to use the conveyor belt in the manufacturing process.

The assembly line reduced the time needed to put together a car from 12 hours to 93 minutes. In 1908, Ford said that his goal was to produce a car a minute. By 1920, he had achieved his goal. A car rolled off his assembly line every minute of the working day. By 1925, the Ford Motor Company was producing cars at the rate of one car every 10 seconds!

The assembly line dramatically reduced the cost of producing cars. As production costs dropped, the price of cars dropped. By 1924, the price was down to $290 per car. Naturally, this created a greater demand for automobiles. In 1916, 600,000 were produced; in 1924, two million rolled off the assembly line.

Some assembly-line work is still being done by people, though much of it is now performed by robots and computers.

AUTOMOBILE SALES IN THE UNITED STATES, 1900–1990	
Year	Number of cars sold
1900	4,192
1910	181,000
1920	1,905,500
1930	2,787,456
1940	3,717,385
1950	6,665,863
1960	6,674,796
1970	6,546,817
1980	8,979,000
1990	6,049,749

By reducing the time needed to produce a car, other costs— production and selling price—were reduced as well. Cars became affordable by vast numbers of people.

Manufacturing on the Move

The moving assembly line brought about great changes, not only in the American automobile industry. Other industries quickly adapted the assembly line to their needs. Bicycles, refrigerators, washing machines, and radios were mass-produced on assembly lines. Assembly lines had made mass production possible. And mass production had made more goods more affordable to more people. The result was a booming economy in the 1920s.

Keeping Workers Happy The assembly line was great for everyone— except factory workers. Because each worker did only one small task over and over again, day after day, the work was extremely monotonous. It required speed but little skill, and workers could take little pride in their accomplishments. Turnover was high, as disgruntled assembly line workers left their jobs after only a short time.

Henry Ford had an answer for worker dissatisfaction, too. In 1914, he raised the salary for Ford Motor Company workers to $5 a day. It was double the standard rate, but Ford could afford it. Even with the raise, he was still making a large profit because the assembly line was saving him so much money in production costs.

Pleased with their raise, Ford workers remained on the job. To hold on to their employees, other auto manufacturers followed his lead. This was the start of a long trend toward high wages and generous benefits in the automobile industry. That trend was continued by the United Automobile Workers, a labor union formed in 1935.

The Assembly Line Today Salary and benefits can only partly compensate for the drudgery of assembly-line jobs. In recent years, manufacturing industries have attempted to avoid worker dissatisfaction by adapting assembly-line principles to a team-centered approach. Manufacturers hope that this will increase the workers' involvement in their jobs and result in a better product for consumers.

33

Rocket

An old flying machine received a new life and took off into space.

In 1926, American physicist Robert Goddard launched the first liquid-fuel rocket. It marked the first major step in landing a human on the moon.

The Rockets' Red Glare

The Chinese took the first step toward space travel when they invented gunpowder in the 10th century. By 1232, they were shooting "arrows of fire" (probably primitive rockets) at the invading Mongols.

Gunpowder rockets were used in Europe by the 14th century. When guns and artillery became more accurate, rockets dropped out of use. However, the British relied on them to defeat Denmark in 1807, Napoleon at Leipzig in 1813, and untrained American militia in 1814. Francis Scott Key wrote the American national anthem—"The Star-Spangled Banner"—while watching the "rockets' red glare."

Looking Ahead Around 1500, a Chinese visionary, Wan-Hu, predicted the use of rockets for space travel. Unfortunately, when he tried to fly to the moon by tying 47 rockets to a chair, he was incinerated.

In 1903, another visionary, Russian schoolteacher and physicist Konstantin Tsiolkovsky, published his ideas on the use of rockets for space travel. Tsiolkovsky described space suits, satellites, the colonization of planets, and a system of propelling rockets by burning liquid fuel. However, he built no rockets.

Many countries have joined the space race. France's *Ariane* rocket is shown here on a launch pad in French Guiana.

Rockets in War and Peace

Until March 16, 1926, all rockets used solid fuel, such as gunpowder. On that day, American scientist Robert Goddard stood in a snow-covered field in Auburn, Massachusetts, and launched the first liquid-fuel rocket. The rocket was about four feet tall and six inches in diameter, and it traveled 200 feet in the air. Although that may not seem far, it was the first important step toward the moon.

Solid fuels like gunpowder depend on the atmosphere for oxygen. Since there is no oxygen beyond the earth's atmosphere, solid-fuel rockets were incapable of space travel. But Goddard's liquid-fuel rocket contained liquid oxygen. Therefore, it was capable of burning beyond the earth's atmosphere. The liquid fuel was also more powerful and could be controlled better than solid fuel.

Von Braun and the V-2 The next developments in rocketry occurred in Germany to fill the needs of the German military during World War II. The leader of the German rocket team was Wernher von Braun, who had become interested in space travel as a teenager. In 1942, von Braun, using the work of Goddard and others, developed the world's first long-range guided missile, the V-2. The missile rose to a height of 60 miles and flew 120 miles at a speed of 3,000 miles per hour. It was first launched militarily against the city of Paris, France, on September 6, 1944. Two days later, Germany pelted London with a thousand V-2s.

By the time the V-2 was in use, von Braun had been arrested by the Nazis and accused of developing rockets for space travel and of having no interest in them as weapons. At the end of the war, he and his team surrendered to the United States. He was brought to this country, where he continued his research, eventually under the direction of the National Aeronautics and Space Administration (NASA). Other German rocket scientists went to work for the Soviet Union.

The Race for Space

The V-2 guided missile was the forerunner of powerful and advanced Soviet and American rockets. Soon after the end of World War II, the Soviet Union and the United States—formerly allies but now Cold War enemies—began a race for space. The Soviets scored a number of significant "firsts."

On October 4, 1957, the Soviets used a rocket to launch *Sputnik 1,* the first human-made satellite placed in orbit around the earth. On October 21, they launched *Sputnik 2,* which carried the first live passenger into space, a dog named Laika. In April 1961, the Soviets sent a man into space. Cosmonaut Yuri Gagarin made one orbit around the earth in *Vostok 1.*

Embarrassed at having been beaten into space, the United States government established NASA in 1958 and appropriated huge amounts of money for the space race. In May 1961, the United States sent astronaut Alan Shepard into space on a suborbital flight. And early in 1962, astronaut John Glenn orbited the earth in *Friendship 7.*

To the Moon The real prize in the space race, however, was the moon. The Americans dominated this race. In 1966, the United States successfully landed research equipment on the moon. In 1968, a manned spaceship orbited the moon. Finally, on July 20, 1969, *Apollo 11* astronauts Neil Armstrong and Edward Aldrin in the detached lunar module *Eagle* touched down on the moon. The message went back to earth, "The *Eagle* has landed." Armstrong descended the ladder from the module to the moon's surface. As he took his first cautious step on lunar soil, he uttered those now-familiar words "That's one small step for man, one giant leap for mankind."

In Space Today the skies are crowded with rocket-launched man-made satellites. They are used for communications, meteorology, and military purposes. Unmanned space flights have gone far beyond the moon. *Voyager 2,* launched in 1977, has flown by Jupiter, Saturn, Uranus, and Neptune sending information about these planets back to Earth.

Several U.S. space flights—with and without crews—are planned for this decade. These include flights to acquire radar images of Earth's surface (1993), to study Saturn (1995), and to collect soil samples from Mars (2000).

In this painting a *Voyager* spacecraft is shown in its flight across the solar system to Jupiter and Saturn. The sun, Mercury, Venus, Earth, and Mars are also shown.

Television

Radio and pictures were combined to produce a powerful tool of mass communication.

Faster and Faster

Imagine your country at war. The enemy has invaded. They've even burned parts of your capital city. Diplomats from your country have sailed across the ocean to try to negotiate peace. Eventually, a ship brings the news that a treaty was signed weeks ago. All the fighting since then has been unnecessary.

This actually happened during the War of 1812 between the United States and Britain. Because ships were the only means of bringing news across the ocean, soldiers fought and died after the peace treaty had been signed.

For thousands of years information traveled by land or by sea. News from distant places was always old news. Then in 1844, Samuel F. B. Morse patented his telegraph, a device that enabled people to send electric signals long distances over wires. Instant communication became a reality.

The telegraph was essentially a tool for private communication. However, Marconi's invention of the wireless, or radio, in 1901 laid the groundwork for the age of mass communication. By the middle of the 1930s, radio broadcasts were a major source of news and entertainment for many American families.

Sound and Picture

As with most modern inventions, there wasn't just one genius working to combine pictures and sound. Scottish inventor John Baird sold shoe polish and razor blades to finance his research. He was trying to find a way to transmit live pictures. In 1925, his efforts paid off when he transmitted the first television image in his attic workshop. His subject was a boy from the office downstairs.

Unfortunately, Baird's invention was obsolete before he even got started. His system was mechanical rather than electronic, and the picture quality was poor. It was only a short time before someone came up with a better idea. That person was the Russian-American inventor Vladimir Zworykin.

The Iconoscope and the Kinescope After Zworykin arrived in the United States, he went to work for the Westinghouse Electric Company, which was doing radio research. At

Russian-born American Vladimir Zworykin held patents for the iconoscope (the first television scanning camera) and the kinescope (the television picture tube).

first he had trouble convincing people that pictures could be sent by radio. But eventually he got the support he needed to continue the research he had begun in Russia. In 1923, Zworykin patented the first television camera, which he called an iconoscope. A year later, he patented a television picture tube—a receiver called a kinescope. These two devices were the basis of the first electronic television system.

Zworykin's research interested David Sarnoff, then vice-president of the Radio Corporation of America (RCA). Sarnoff persuaded Zworykin to move to RCA, where he was given a team of researchers to work on his ideas.

Scientists in Great Britain were also experimenting with television. In 1936, the first commercial television transmission took place in England over the British Broadcasting Corporation (BBC). Later that same year, RCA began regular broadcasts in the United States.

Television was not an immediate sensation. The first sets were expensive and offered a pretty poor picture on a very small screen—about five inches. And there were only a few programs for viewing. Then, when the United States entered World War II in 1941, all resources were allocated to producing necessary war materials. So it wasn't until the late 1940s that television began to have an impact.

◀ Television was not an immediate sensation, though it was a curiosity. In 1953, people in New York watched the coronation of Queen Elizabeth II, which was taking place in England.

Gigantic television screens at the 1992 Olympic Games in Barcelona gave spectators a close-up view of the action.

The Age of Television

Advances in the late 1940s made television more popular. The electronic equipment in televisions became more compact, making sets less bulky. In the 1950s, the screen expanded to 21 inches, and picture quality improved greatly. In 1954, viewers saw the first color broadcast. Most importantly, the amount and variety of programming had increased significantly. Many popular radio shows switched to television. Live television dramas showcased the talents of the finest actors from stage and screen. Comedians like "Uncle Miltie" (Milton Berle) entertained the public weekly. Children tuned in every weekday night to see a freckle-faced puppet named Howdy Doody.

The number of American homes containing television sets grew steadily until 1978, when 97 percent of families in the United States had at least one television.

Vast Wasteland or Not? For almost half a century, television has strongly influenced people's lives, and the debate concerning the influence of television has raged for decades. On the positive side, television has provided vast amounts of up-to-the-minute news and information. But critics have said that too much of the programming is mindless, or worse, harmful. In 1961, Newton Minow, chairman of the Federal Communications Commission, called television a "vast wasteland." Many still agree with that view. Parents worry that their children see too much violence and sex on television. Political commentators are concerned that political campaigns geared to television emphasize style and appearance over substance.

In 1969, Congress established the Public Broadcasting System (PBS) to provide more educational programs, such as "Sesame Street," classic films, in-depth news shows, and how-to programs. But PBS is only partially funded by the government and must constantly fight for financial survival.

One recent development in television programming has been cable television. By offering viewers more channels and more specialized programs, cable companies have broken up the monopolies that the three major networks held for so long.

Another development is the establishment of an information network that combines television, computers, and telephone lines. Subscribers can use the system to pay bills, buy airline tickets, and monitor checking and credit card accounts.

Nuclear Fission

A new source of energy is capable of producing electricity and immensely destructive weapons.

▼ Fermi won the Nobel Prize in physics in 1938. His work marked the beginning of the nuclear age.

▶ The first nuclear chain reaction was observed by Fermi and his colleagues in a squash court at the University of Chicago.

The Powerful Nucleus

Throughout history, people have developed increasingly powerful and impersonal ways to kill each other. Nuclear weapons are the latest. They get their power from a process called nuclear fission. The nucleus, or central part, of an atom has the potential to produce vast amounts of energy. The energy is released when the atom is split, or undergoes fission. The split nucleus yields a smaller particle called a neutron. The neutron can cause a self-sustaining chain reaction as it, in turn, splits new atoms. If the reaction is controlled, it generates nuclear power and electricity. If it is uncontrolled, it produces nuclear explosions.

Einstein's Famous Theory The long march toward nuclear warfare began back in 1905, when Albert Einstein formulated his theory of relativity. According to Einstein, matter is a form of energy and energy is a form of matter. Einstein's famous equation $E = mc^2$ describes the relationship between matter and energy. During nuclear fission, the splitting of an atom, a very small amount of matter is replaced by an immense amount of energy.

The Ultimate Bomb

In the late 1930s, as Hitler's Germany prepared to go to war, two German scientists, Otto Hahn and Fritz Strassmann, were close to harnessing the power of nuclear fission. Although the two did not fully understand the implications of their experiments, they communicated their findings to Lise Meitner, a colleague who had fled to Denmark to escape Nazi oppression. Meitner and her nephew, Otto Frisch, understood what Hahn and Strassmann did not. Their conclusions were soon communicated to scientists in the United States, including Enrico Fermi, an Italian physicist, who had conducted his own important atomic studies in the 1930s. Fermi had left Italy in 1938 and became an American citizen in 1944.

Fermi and others in the United States feared what might happen if Germany unlocked the secret of nuclear fission: atomic bombs could be unleashed on the world by the militant Nazi nation. They persuaded Albert Einstein to sign a letter to President Franklin Roosevelt describing the danger.

The forceful letter convinced Roosevelt, and the U.S. government

poured massive amounts of money into developing a nuclear bomb before Germany. The top-secret Manhattan Project, headed by physicist J. Robert Oppenheimer, recruited the best scientists in the country to work on the all-out effort.

Working for the project, Enrico Fermi built the first nuclear reactor in Chicago, and in December 1942, he produced the first controlled chain reaction. The government received word of the success of his experiment in a coded telegram that read, "The Italian navigator has landed in the New World."

Once a chain reaction had been achieved, the Manhattan Project scientists rapidly developed a bomb. On July 14, 1945, the first nuclear bomb was tested in the New Mexico desert. In an attempt to halt continued Japanese aggression and hoping to end World War II quickly, an atomic bomb was dropped on Hiroshima, Japan, on August 6. Three days later, a second bomb was dropped on another Japanese city, Nagasaki. Japan soon surrendered to the Allies. Ironically, it was learned later that Germany had given up work on nuclear fission in June of 1942, believing that nuclear weapons were not possible.

A Nuclear Future?

The world was stunned by the terrible destruction at Hiroshima and Nagasaki. Over 200,000 people were killed. Others were permanently disfigured or disabled by radiation burns and radiation sickness, the inevitable results of nuclear fallout. But the destruction and pain did not stop the stockpiling of nuclear bombs.

The Soviet Union, a wartime ally of the United States, quickly turned into a peacetime enemy. When the Soviet Union tested its first nuclear bomb in 1949, debate flared in the United States about whether to invest in an even more destructive bomb—a hydrogen bomb, fueled by nuclear fusion, the energy created by combining atoms. Robert Oppenheimer, having seen the bitter fruits of his work, opposed the new bomb, but he lost the debate, and it cost him his career. To this day, although there has been some progress toward nuclear disarmament, the peace between heavily armed superpowers remains an uneasy one.

What Benefits?   After the war, scientists also turned their attention to the possible benefits of nuclear fission as a source of nuclear energy.

The first nuclear reactor to produce electricity was built in England in 1953. The Soviet Union followed in 1954, and the United States in 1957.

However, nuclear energy, at first seen as a cleaner and cheaper alternative to fossil fuels, has been the center of great controversy. In 1979, a partial meltdown of the reactor core and the release of radioactive gases at the Three Mile Island nuclear power plant near Harrisburg, Pennsylvania, underscored the potential danger of nuclear accidents. Severe radiation sickness from nuclear fallout could result from accidents at nuclear power stations as well as from nuclear explosions. As people became aware of this and the problems of disposing of nuclear wastes, the construction of nuclear energy plants in the United States came to a complete halt. Whether the United States will once again permit the building of nuclear reactors remains unclear. Many are still operating, providing electricity to Americans. Disposing of radioactive waste from these power plants remains an unsolved problem.

In other countries, such as France and the former Soviet Union, concern about fallout developed more slowly than in the United States. That is, until 1986, when a nuclear accident occurred at the Chernobyl plant near the Ukrainian city of Kiev. The area is still too radioactive to allow people to return to their homes. And it is still too soon to determine how far-reaching and long-lasting the effects will be.

Having seen the terrible effects of the atomic bomb, Oppenheimer said that "it made the prospect of . . . war unendurable."

Computer

An electronic machine performs a wide variety of operations in fractions of a second.

ENIAC, the first fully electronic computer, was like a large dinosaur with limited usefulness.

Drowning in Paper

As recently as the 1970s, the typical business office was awash in paper. Overstuffed file cabinets lined the walls. Although adding machines were available for simple mathematical calculations, most office work—inventory control, record keeping, payroll, billing, reports—was done in pencil and finalized on typewriters that noisily clacked away all day. One slip of the typist's finger could mean redoing whole pages of work. Think of the savings in time and effort if a machine could perform some of these tasks automatically and without making errors.

The Analytical Engine More than a century ago, in 1822, an Englishman named Charles Babbage recognized the need for such a machine—especially in the area of mathematical computations. Babbage began work on his analytical engine, a steam-driven machine intended to store and retrieve information submitted on punched cards and to print out answers. Although he worked on developing his machine for nearly 50 years, he ultimately failed. His ideas were sound, but the technology of the day was inadequate to the task.

ENIAC to PCs

Babbage's analytical engine was the forerunner of today's computers. Computers are machines with electronic memories that are able to store instructions and information. The instructions, called computer programs, tell the computer what to do with certain information. For example, one simple type of computer is a calculator, a device programmed with mathematical rules. When information—a math problem—is keyed in, the computer uses the rules in its memory to solve the problem.

Although several people after Babbage devised machines to do mathematical calculations, the modern computer dates back to 1946, when the United States Army built the first fully electronic computer, called ENIAC (electronic numerical integrator and calculator). Designed by J. P. Eckert and J. W. Mauchly, ENIAC weighed 30 tons and took up 1,500 square feet of space. It was controlled by vacuum tubes and could perform about 5,000 operations per second. However, ENIAC produced enormous amounts of heat, and its valves had to rest periodically.

Milestones in the Development of the Computer

1944 Aiken invents Mark I, an electronic computer using relay switches.

1946 Two engineers invent ENIAC, a fully electronic computer using vacuum tubes.

1951 ENIAC inventors build UNIVAC, which handles alphabetic and numeric data.

1958 The integrated circuit is created, enabling computers to process data faster and become smaller.

1971 Microprocessor is invented.

1978 First personal computer (PC) is built.

1988 Notebook-sized computers become available.

1991 Clipboard computers are introduced; keyboard is replaced with a liquid screen and electronic stylus.

Through the Generations ENIAC was part of the so-called first generation of mainframe computers. Since ENIAC, the trend has been to more powerful computers packed into smaller spaces.

In 1948, the invention of the transistor paved the way for the second generation of computers—smaller, faster, and less expensive than ENIAC and its contemporaries.

In the mid-1960s, miniaturized integrated circuits replaced transistors, leading to the third generation of computers—minicomputers and high-speed mainframes with huge memory capacities.

The invention of the silicon chip ushered in the fourth generation of computers. They were smaller, more powerful, and more affordable than any before them. A silicon chip is no bigger than a fingernail, yet it can store millions of bits of information. By 1978, silicon chips had facilitated the development of the personal computer (PC), now a fixture in most offices and in many homes.

Telephone operators use computers to find numbers. Computers have simplified many tasks, and created new jobs—for programmers and data processors.

This tiny chip made computers faster and increased their memory capacity.

The Computer Age

Today computers are everywhere: schools, homes, offices, stores, libraries. And, with the new laptops and electronic notebooks, computers even travel. About 40 percent of the workers in industrialized countries use computers in their work. In many offices, computers have replaced typewriters, adding machines, and file cabinets. With a computer, office workers can write and edit memos, letters, and reports, correcting errors before they print them. With computers, financial workers can perform numerous mathematical calculations in seconds. And with computers, people can sort through and store reams of data.

Computers are also in factories, guiding precision operations. In shoe manufacturing, computers are now used to design and make patterns for shoes. Make an airline reservation, place a phone call, or withdraw money from a bank account. Chances are, a computer will be involved in the transaction. There are computers in automobile fuel control systems and in traffic lights. And computers are replacing the old card catalogs in most libraries.

Computers Come Home The increasing number of home computers has made it possible for more people to work at home instead of at the office, either part time or full time.

Home computers are also being used for entertainment, banking, games, and shopping. Even if you don't have a home computer, you probably have a computer in your home. Computers help operate compact disk players, digital watches and clocks, microwave ovens, and video games.

The Next Generation Like all past computers, today's computers are only as good as the programs a human being puts into them. One small error in a computer program can make the computer's output worthless. The next generation of computers may be able to avoid this problem by using artificial intelligence to correct and improve its own programs.

Laser

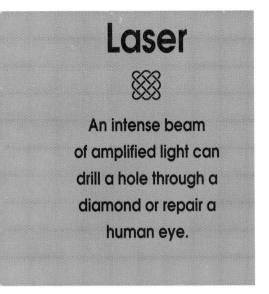

An intense beam of amplified light can drill a hole through a diamond or repair a human eye.

▶ The use of laser scanning in supermarkets helps managers keep track of prices, inventory, and sales.

Albert Einstein was the first to describe the principle of the laser.

It All Began with Einstein

As with so much of modern science, the groundwork for lasers was laid by Albert Einstein (1879–1955). Recognized now as one of the greatest physicists of all time, Einstein came to the United States in the early 1930s. The Nazis had revoked his German citizenship because he was Jewish.

In 1917, Einstein published a paper in which he described the principle of the laser (for *light amplification by stimulated emission of radiation*). He said that when light of a specific wavelength hits an atom that is highly excited, the atom will give off light of the same wavelength, or color. This intensifies the original light. Ordinary light is *chaotic:* it occurs in numerous wavelengths and scatters in all directions. Laser light, however, is *coherent.* The rays are all the same wavelength (producing a very pure color), and they move in the same direction to produce a beam of great intensity.

Masers For many years, no one was able to translate Einstein's theory into any practical application. However, from the mid-1930s to the early 1950s—just before, during, and after World War II—there was much interest in the military possibilities of radar (radio waves that detect an object at a distance). After the war, microwaves became important to the study of radar and radio astronomy. The term *microwave* refers to that part of the electromagnetic spectrum associated with the longer infrared waves and the shorter radio waves.

One of the scientists studying microwaves was American physicist Charles Townes. In 1953, he applied Einstein's early theories to microwaves and developed a device that produced an intense beam of microwaves with rays all of the same wavelength. Townes called his discovery *microwave amplification by stimulated emission of radiation,* or *maser,* for short.

At about the same time, two scientists from the Soviet Union, Aleksandr Mikhaylovich Prokhorov and Nikolay Gennadiyevich Basov, also worked out the theory of the maser. In 1964, the three scientists shared the Nobel Prize in physics.

Maser to Laser

After his success with the maser, Charles Townes put forth the theory that a laser could be built. Townes and a colleague tried to build a laser using potassium vapor, but their attempts failed.

Then, in 1960, American physicist Theodore Maiman did produce the first working laser. His device was a ruby rod that he flooded with high-intensity light from a flash lamp. The result was a beam of red light. One end of the ruby rod was covered with a silver film, and the other end was partially silvered. The light given off by the ruby was reflected back and forth between the two ends, producing an even more intense laser light from the partly silvered end. The concentrated light was able to drill a hole through a diamond.

In 1962, to demonstrate the intensity of laser light, scientists aimed a laser beam at the moon. When it reached the moon—240,000 miles away—it had spread to an area only 2 miles wide.

Putting Lasers to Work

At first, the laser was called the invention with no use. But that didn't last long. Within 30 years of its discovery, scientists had found numerous practical applications for the laser. If you've ever gone through an automated checkout counter at a supermarket or listened to a compact disk, you've experienced the power of lasers.

Serious Lasers In the field of medicine, surgeons use lasers to perform such delicate procedures as eye operations and brain surgery. Lasers can also be used to reduce inflammation and pain in some patients. Researchers are developing laser techniques to help physicians perform arterial surgery, destroy kidney and bladder stones, and remove spinal cord tumors.

Industries use lasers to cut almost any material, from ceramics to rubber to cloth. Telephone companies use lasers to carry information over very fine glass fibers (fiber optics). Since glass is cheaper than copper—the original component of telephone wires—and since lasers can carry huge amounts of information, fiber optics greatly increase the capacity of telephone communications systems.

Supermarkets use lasers to scan the bar codes on products to register the prices of items when customers check out. The computer industry uses lasers in its newest and most efficient printers. The first printers were as noisy as typewriters and typed about one line per second. Laser printers, developed in 1982 by IBM, work more quickly and quietly than standard printers. They print about 30 lines per second.

Fun Lasers The entertainment industry has found many ways to use lasers to create exciting new visual effects. Designers use lasers to create stunning outdoor displays and to provide background light shows for rock concerts.

Lasers are also used to produce holograms—three-dimensional moving photographs that simulate reality. In 1972, the recording industry found a way to use laser beams to record music on compact disks. This method produces a sound that is much closer to perfection than was ever produced with tape or record players. Compact disks have two additional advantages: more sound can be recorded than on a record or tape, and compact disks never wear out.

Lasers enable physicians to perform delicate and complicated surgery that previously was too risky.

Glossary

aerodynamics: The study of the motion of air and other gases and of forces acting on bodies moving in air.

artificial intelligence: The ability of computers to imitate human reasoning functions.

assembly line: A line of workers, machines, and equipment in a factory along which a product passes until it is completely assembled.

bacteria (sing. bacterium): One-celled microorganisms, some of which can cause disease.

Bakelite: A synthetic resin or plastic made from phenol and formaldehyde.

camera obscura: A room or box with a hole (sometimes containing a lens) in one wall through which light is projected onto the opposite wall, forming an image of what is outside.

celluloid: A flammable substance made from pyroxylin and camphor; considered the first plastic.

chain reaction: A continuous series of nuclear fission reactions.

combine: A harvesting machine that both reaps and threshes grain.

conveyor belt: A continuous moving belt that transports objects from place to place.

daguerreotype: An early photograph printed on a silver-coated copper plate.

diaphragm: An adjustable opening that controls the amount of light passing through the lens of a camera.

fiber optics: Very thin glass or plastic fibers that transmit light and can be used to carry much more information than ordinary wires.

fossil fuels: Fuels formed from the remains of prehistoric plants and animals; examples are coal, oil, and natural gas.

incandescent lamp: A lamp in which light is produced by electrically heating a thin wire called a filament inside a glass bulb.

integrated circuit: A grouping of many transistor circuits on one plate.

interchangeable parts: A system for mass production in manufacturing in which a given part is always the same size, so that it can be replaced with the same part from another product.

internal-combustion engine: An engine in which fuel is burned inside the engine itself rather than in a separate furnace, as in a steam engine.

laser (light amplification by stimulated emission of radiation): A device that concentrates light into a narrow, intense beam.

locomotive: An engine that can move under its own power, used for pulling railroad cars.

maser (microwave amplification by stimulated emission of radiation): A device that produces a concentrated beam of microwaves.

microwaves: Electromagnetic radiation with a wavelength between one millimeter and one meter—slightly shorter than most radio waves and slightly longer than infrared radiation.

Morse code: A system that uses patterns of dots and dashes to represent letters of the alphabet.

nuclear fallout: Radioactive particles falling to earth after a nuclear explosion.

nuclear fission: The splitting of an atomic nucleus, which releases energy.

nuclear fusion: The energy created by combining atoms.

nuclear reactor: A device in which controlled nuclear fission reactions can be produced.

pasteurization: The treatment of food with heat to destroy disease-causing organisms.

radar (radio detecting and ranging): A system that uses reflected radio waves to detect distant objects.

radiation sickness: Sickness caused by overexposure to radiation, such as X rays or nuclear fallout.

reaper: A machine that harvests grain by cutting the stalks.

rocket: A vehicle in which the burning of fuel expels gases from the rear, driving the rocket forward by the principle of reaction (Newton's third law of motion).

satellite: A natural or artificial object revolving about another object in space.

silicon chip: A tiny integrated circuit that can contain millions of bits of information.

telegraph: A system for transmitting messages by sending electric signals over wires.

threshing machine: A machine that separates grain from its husks by beating.

transistor: A small electronic device that replaced the vacuum tube in radios and computers.

treadle: A lever operated with the foot.

Suggested Readings

Note: An asterisk (*) denotes a Young Adult title.

Amato, Carol J. *Inventions.* Smithmark Publishers, 1992.

Bertolotti, Mario. *Masers and Lasers: An Historical Approach.* American Institute of Physics, 1983.

Boettinger, H. M. *The Telephone Book: Bell, Watson, Vail and American Life, 1876–1983.* Stearn Publishers Ltd., 1983.

*Cumming, David. *Photography.* Raintree Steck-Vaughn, 1989.

Diebold, John. *The Innovators.* NAL-Dutton, 1990.

Flatow, Ira. *They All Laughed . . . From Light Bulbs to Lasers, the Fascinating Stories Behind the Great Inventions That Have Changed Our Lives.* HarperCollins, 1992.

Godfrey, Frank P. *International History of the Sewing Machine.* Trans-Atlantic Publications, 1982.

Goldberg, Vicki. *The Power of Photography: How Photographs Changed Our Lives.* Abbeville Press, 1991.

Graetzerk, Hans G. *The Discovery of Nuclear Fission.* Ayers and Company, 1981.

*Graham, Ian. *Communications.* Raintree Steck-Vaughn, 1991.

*———. *Transportation.* Raintree Steck-Vaughn, 1993.

Greenia, Mark W. *Computers and Computing: A Chronology of the People and Machines That Made Computer History.* Lexikon Services, 1990.

Hills, Richard L. *Power from Steam: A History of the Stationary Steam Engine.* Cambridge University Press, 1989.

Inglis, Andrew F. *Behind the Tube: History of Broadcasting.* Focal Press, 1990.

*Jefferis, David. *Flight.* Franklin Watts, 1991.

*Kurland, Gerald. *Henry Ford: Pioneer in the Automotive Industry.* Sam Har Press, 1972.

Lattu, Kristan R. *History of Rocketry and Astronautics.* Univelt Inc., 1989.

MacDonald, Anne L. *Feminine Ingenuity: Women and Invention in America.* Ballantine Books, 1992.

Monk, Lorraine. *Photographs That Changed the World.* Doubleday and Company, 1989.

Newhouse, Elizabeth L. *Inventors and Discoverers: Changing Our World.* National Geographic Society, 1988.

*Olney, Ross R. *The Farm Combine.* Walker and Company, 1984.

Panati, Charles. *Breakthroughs.* Berkeley Books, 1981.

Sears, Stephen W. *The American Heritage History of the Automobile in America.* Simon & Schuster, 1977.

Siegel, Beatrice. *The Steam Engine.* Walker and Company, 1986.

Stoiko, Michael. *Pioneers of Rocketry.* Amereon Ltd., 1985.

Taylor, Michael. *History of Flight.* Outlet Book Company, 1991.

*Turvey, Peter. *Inventors and Ingenious Ideas.* Franklin Watts, 1992.

Vare, Ethlie Ann. *Mothers of Invention: A History of Forgotten Women.* William Morrow and Company, 1988.

White, John H., Jr. *A History of the American Locomotive, 1830–1880.* Dover Publications, 1980.

Williams, Trevor I. *The History of Invention: From Stone Axes to Silicon Chips.* Facts on File, 1987.

World of Inventions. Gale Research, 1993.

Index

Adams, Ansel, 13
Ader, Clément, 30
Aeolipile, 4
Air-conditioning, 19
Airplane, 30–31
Aldrin, Edward, 35
Alexander Graham Bell Association
    for the Deaf, 23
American Telephone and Telegraph
    Company (AT&T), 23
Apollo 11 (spacecraft), 35
Appert, Nicolas, 6
Armstrong, Neil, 35
Assembly line, 27, **32–33**
Atomic bomb, 38–39
Automobile, 26–27, 32–33

Babbage, Charles, 40
Baekeland, Leo, 21
Baird, John, 36
Bakelite, 21
Basov, Nikolay Gennadiyevich, 42
Bell, Alexander Graham, 22–23
Bell Telephone Company, 23
Benz, Karl Friedrich, 26, 27
Best Friend of Charleston (locomo-
    tive), 11
Billiard balls, plastic for, 20–21
Birdseye, Clarence, 19
Boeing 247, 31
Bonaparte, Napoleon, 6
Brady, Matthew, 13
British Broadcasting Corporation
    (BBC), 37

Cable television, 37
Calculator, 40
Camera, 12–13
Camera obscura, 12
Canning, 6–7
Carothers, Wallace Hume, 21
Carrier, Willis, 19
Cayley, George, 30
CBS, 29
Celluloid, 21
Central Pacific Railroad, 11
Chlorofluorocarbons, 19
Cold War, 35
Collodion, 20

Combine harvester, 14–15
Communication
    lasers and, 43
    radio and, 28–29
    telephone and, 22–23, 43
    television and, 36–37
Compact disks, 43
Computer, 40–41, 43
Concorde (aircraft), 31
Conservation of fuel, 21
Conveyor belts, 32–33
Corporations, 11
Cotton gin, 8
Cugnot, Nicholas-Joseph, 5, 26
Cullen, William, 18
Curtis, Edward, 13

Daguerre, Louis, 12, 13
Daguerreotypes, 12–13
Davy, Humphrey, 24
De Forest, Lee, 28
Donkin, Bryan, 6
Donkin and Hall, 6
Duryea, Charles E., 26
Duryea, J. Frank, 26

Eagle (lunar module), 35
Eastman, George, 13, 21
Eckert, J. P., 40
Edison, Thomas Alva, 23, 25
Edison and Swan United Electric
    Light Company, 25
Einstein, Albert, 38, 42
Electric light, 24–25
England, 5, 11, 19, 39
ENIAC, 40–41
Entertainment, 29, 43

Factories
    assembly line and, 27, 32–33
    computers in, 41
    Industrial Revolution and, 5
    interchangeable parts and, 8–9
    lasers in, 43
Faraday, Michael, 24
Fermi, Enrico, 38, 39
Fessenden, Reginald, 28
Fiber optics, 43
Film (photographic), 13, 21

Fluorescent lighting, 25
Flyer (aircraft), 31
Flyer III (aircraft), 31
Food
    refrigeration of, 18–19
    spoilage of, 6
    transporting, 19
Food canning, 6–7
Ford, Henry, 26, 27, 32, 33
Ford Motor Company, 32–33
Freon, 19
Friendship 7 (spacecraft), 35
Frisch, Otto, 38

Gagarin, Yuri, 35
General Electric Company, 25
General Motors, 27
Germany, 35, 38, 39
Glenn, John, 35
Goddard, Robert, 34
Gray, Elisha, 23
Great Exhibition (London, 1851), 9
Gun manufacture, 8–9, 32

Hahn, Otto, 38
Harrison, James, 18–19
Hero (Greek scientist), 4
Hertz, Heinrich, 28
Hiroshima, Japan, 39
Holograms, 43
Howe, Elias, 17
Hubbard, Gardiner G., 23
Hunt, Walter, 17
Hyatt, John Wesley, 20–21
Hydrogen bomb, 39

Icebox, 18, 19
Iconoscope, 37
Incandescent light, 24–25
Industrial Revolution, 5, 9
Information network, 37
Integrated circuits, 41
Interchangeable parts, 8–9

Japan, 39
Jet aircraft, 31

Keller, Helen, 23
Kinescope, 37

Labor movement, 11
Laser, 42–43
Latimer, Lewis H., 25
Light
   electric, 24–25
   lasers and, 42–43
Lilienthal, Otto, 30
Lindbergh, Charles, 31
Linde, Karl von, 19
Liverpool and Manchester Railway, 11
Locomotive, 10–11

McCormick, Cyrus, 15
McCormick, Robert, 15
Maiman, Theodore, 43
Manhattan Project, 39
Marconi, Guglielmo, 28, 36
Maser, 42–43
Massey-Harris, 15
Mass production, 8–9, 17, 27, 32–33
Mauchly, J. W., 40
Maxwell, James Clerk, 13
MBS (Mutual Broadcasting System), 29
Medicine, lasers in, 43
Meikle, Andrew, 15
Meitner, Lise, 38
Microwaves, 42
Midgley, Thomas, 19
Model T, 27, 32
Moon landing, 35
Moore, A. Y., 15
Morse, Samuel F. B., 22, 36
Morse code, 22
Moving assembly line, 27, 32–33
Murrow, Edward R., 29

National Aeronautics and Space Administration (NASA), 35
Native Americans, 11, 13
NBC, 29
Needham, John Turberville, 6
Neon lights, 25
Newcomen, Thomas, 4–5
Niepce, Joseph-Nicéphore, 12
Nuclear fission, 38–39
Nylon, 21

Oersted, Hans Christian, 24
Olds, Ransom E., 32
Oldsmobile, 32
Oppenheimer, J. Robert, 39
Otto, Nikolaus, 26

Pasteur, Louis, 7
Pasteurization, 7
Patents, 8, 17, 21, 23, 25
Pearl Street power station, 25
Perkins, Jacob, 18
Personal computer (PC), 41
Phelan and Collender, 20
Photography, 12–13, 20
Plastics, 20–21
Prokhorov, Aleksandr Mikhaylovich, 42
Public Broadcasting System (PBS), 37
Pyroxylin, 20–21

Radar, 42
Radio, 28–29, 36
Radio Corporation of America (RCA), 37
Railroads, 10–11
Reaper, 14–15
Refrigeration, 18–19
Reis, Philip, 22
Relativity, theory of, 38
Riis, Jacob, 13
Rocket, 34–35
Rocket (locomotive), 10
Roosevelt, Franklin, 38–39

San Francisco–Panama International Exposition (1915), 25
Sarnoff, David, 37
Satellites, 23, 35
Sewing machine, 16–17
Shepard, Alan, 35
Silicon chip, 41
Singer, Isaac M., 17
South Carolina Canal and Rail Road Company, 11
Soviet Union, 35, 39
Space travel, 34, 35
Spallanzani, Lazzaro, 6
Spirit of St. Louis (aircraft), 31
Sprengel, Hermann, 25
Sputnik 1 (satellite), 35
Sputnik 2 (satellite), 35
"Star-Spangled Banner, The" (song), 34
Stationnaire (ship), 6
Steam engine, 4–5, 10–11
Stephenson, George, 10
Stephenson, Robert, 10
Stieglitz, Alfred, 13
Strassmann, Fritz, 38
Swan, Joseph, 25

Talbot, W. H. Fox, 13
Telegraph, 22, 36
Telephone, 22–23, 43
Television, 29, **36–37**
Telstar (satellite), 23
Thimonnier, Barthélemy, 16
Three Mile Island accident, 39
Threshing machines, 15
Tin cans, 6–7
Tin Lizzie, 27
Titanic (ship), 28
Townes, Charles, 42, 43
Transistor, 29, 41
Transportation, 10, 19, 26
   by air, 30–31
   by automobile, 19, 26–27
   by rail, 10–11, 26
   rocket and, 34–35
   steam engine and, 5
Trevithick, Richard, 5, 10
Tsiolkovsky, Konstantin, 34

Union Pacific Railroad, 11
Unions, 9, 11, 33
United Automobile Workers, 33

V-2 (guided missile), 35
Velox, 21
Vinci, Leonardo da, 30
Volta, Alessandro, 24
von Braun, Werner, 35
Vostok 1 (spacecraft), 35
Voyager 2 (spacecraft), 35

Wan-Hu, 34
Watson, Thomas A., 23
Watt, James, 5
Wedgwood, Josiah, 12
Wedgwood, Thomas, 12
Westinghouse, George, 11
Westinghouse Electric Company, 36
Whitney, Eli, 8–9, 32
Wilson, Allen Benjamin, 17
World War I, 28, 31
World War II, 29, 31, 35, 38–39
Wright, Orville, 30
Wright, Wilbur, 30

Yeager, Charles, 31

Zworykin, Vladimir, 36–37